The Great Black Swamp III

*further historical tales of
northwest ohio*

by

Jim Mollenkopf

Lake of the Cat Publishing
P.O. Box 351454
Toledo, OH 43635-1454

Printed in the United States of America.

CONTENTS

FOREWORD

It was a fine, September morning on the sun-sparkled waters of Lake Erie in 1813 when British and American warships, their white sails magnificent against a deep blue sky, sailed slowly toward each other in the waters off Put-in-Bay. All was quiet aboard the ships, save for an occasional officer's order or boatswain's whistle. And in what "seemed like the awful silence that precedes an earthquake," according an American seaman, the sailors were alone with their thoughts, contemplating their fate, knowing that very soon some of them would die or suffer terrible wounds.

The two lines of ships drew nearer and nearer in a light breeze and just before noon the strains of music drifted through the air as British musicians played "Rule Britannia." Soon the roar of cannons thundered across the lake, echoing off the Canadian and U.S. shores, and sending settlers on both sides running to water's edge to listen. The Battle of Lake Erie had begun.

The only battle ever fought on Lake Erie was part a series of sometimes chaotic events that took place in the years 1812 and 1813 in northwest Ohio as a result of the War of 1812, the last time war visited this region. And the stories of some of those who were on the front lines of that war appear in this book. Other stories include that of a young, French priest who wandered the Great Black Swamp looking for souls to serve; of the daily lives of area Native Americans; of the journeys of European immigrants who left everything behind to come here; of an American renegade who fought first for the Americans then for the British in the American Revolution and was a staunch Indian ally in the Ohio Indian Wars; of the five forts that were built along the Maumee River between Toledo and Fort Wayne, Indiana; and of a former Toledo street urchin who rose to being a contemporary of Mark Twain before he mysteriously disappeared off the coast of Cuba in 1873.

On a personal note, this volume completes an "unintended trilogy" of books about the Great Black Swamp and other northwest Ohio historical events, an effort that began in 1999. When *The Great Black Swamp* came out that year, I had no idea there would be a *Great Black Swamp II*. Likewise, when that book was released, I never thought there would be a *Great Black Swamp III* but here it is. What I've learned is that buried in the layers of the rich history of northwest Ohio are a lot of stories worth digging out and telling again. In this book as in the previous ones, I've endeavored to use personal accounts and narratives. Although such sources can contain errors in fact and memory, romanticization, and even embellishments, they do provide an idea of the experiences of flesh and blood people who came before us, whether it's in relation to a major historical event or merely just another day in the life.

I would like to thank all of those involved with the gathering and preservation of northwest Ohio history. Of particular help in providing material for this work were the local history and genealogy department of the Toledo-Lucas County Public Library; Sauder Village in Archbold and artist Norma Thomas-Herr; the Williams County Historical Society, Montpelier, and the Fort Meigs Museum and Education Center. Thanks are due as well to Ed Peper and Russ Patterson of Napoleon for providing information on General Robert K. Scott; to Bob Rice of Toledo for providing the diary of his great-great-great-grandmother Anna Hall; and to Kevin Joyce of the Black Swamp Conservancy in Perrysburg for providing information on Forrest Woods Preserve. As in my past books, both the historical journal *Northwest Ohio Quarterly* and access to a statewide borrowing system through the University of Toledo's Carlson Library were invaluable resources.

CHAPTER I

GREAT BLACK SWAMP PRIEST

It was late September 1838, and a young priest in France named Prospectus Joseph Machebeuf meditated, praying for guidance toward a life vocation. At the end of three days he had his answer. He would go to America and minister to the souls in the young country burgeoning there.

The following summer, despite the strong objections of family and friends, he boarded a ship for a voyage to America. As the sun set on the first night he took stock of his fellow passengers. "About sixty passengers are in our part of the ship and the majority of these are Protestants. In the other part of the vessel there are nearly two hundred Germans—men, women and children, a few of whom are merchants, and the rest are of the peasant-farmer class. Among the Germans there are a few Catholics, a great many Protestants, and about forty Jews. This is but a sample of the incredible number of immigrants who are arriving in the United States from all parts."

The 200 or so Germans were all lodged in a single, common room and provided their own food. The ship supplied them only with wood and water. Father Machebeuf, and the missionaries he was traveling with, fared considerably better as they slept six to a room and dined nightly at the captain's table. The young priest generally enjoyed his voyage, even managing to avoid the seasickness that laid low his fellow travelers. Finally the call came from the captain that they all had been awaiting, *Land!* "Now our ship is at anchor and we are going to board a steamer to take us to land," he wrote. "The poor Germans must stay on ship two days to wash and clean up. They have sad need of it! God be a thousand times blessed! We are all now in New York, in good health, after forty-four days of navigation. August 21, 1839."

Traveling from New York by canal and stagecoach, the 25-year-old priest reached Cincinnati in September and after a few weeks was sent by the bishop there to northwest Ohio and the frontier town of Tiffin. In Europe at the time, sending out a young and inexperienced priest alone was unheard of. However Father Machebeuf jumped into his first assignment with both feet and soon set out to visit the other settlements in the area and minister to his far-flung flock, many of whom were scattered about the Great Black Swamp.

He soon traveled from Tiffin down the Sandusky River to Lower Sandusky, now Fremont. There, "I learned that a good number of Canadian farmers had settled on Mud Creek, nine or ten miles down the river. I went there immediately and found over thirty families, mostly from Detroit and Monroe, Mich. A good widow lady gave me a beautiful site for a chapel on the banks of the river and, to make a beginning, I appointed some pious ladies to teach catechism on Sundays and a few days during the week, and promised to visit them every month. To facilitate the keeping of my promise I bought a Canadian pony, on credit, and borrowed a saddle. Thus equipped, I returned to Lower Sandusky where I rested a day and then began the long and tedious journey through the Black Swamp to the Maumee River.

"In the beginning of November 1839, I visited for the first time the Irish laborers working on the National, or macadamized, road then being built through the Black Swamp from Fremont to Perrysburg on the Maumee river." (The road, now U.S. 20, was regarded then as the worst road in America until it was macadamized, or paved with broken stone, beginning in 1838.) "The National Road was graded and partly macadamized but it was very rough and I traveled only a few miles a day. The first day I had only gone five or six miles when I came upon a party of good Irishmen working upon the road."

These Irishmen were practicing Catholics who had not seen a priest for some time and were not going to pass up this opportunity. They made up a story about a sick man needing a priest and led the father to a cabin some distance away. "I found there was no sick man, but that they had perpetuated this pious fraud to keep me for the next day, which was Sunday. I made no objection to this arrangement, for it suited me very well, so on Sunday I set up my little altar and said mass and ventured to say a few words to them in English (Father Machebeuf spoke only French). "After mass I had four or five children to baptize and the generous men were so grateful for the privilege of hearing mass in that wild country and of having their children baptized that they gave me almost enough money to pay for my pony. Promising to visit them on my return, I set out for Perrysburg, rejoicing that I had stopped on Saturday for the 'sick' man.

"At that time Perrysburg was but a poor little village on the east side of the Maumee river. I found there only one Catholic family, poor Canadians, in a little cabin. I said mass for them and then crossed the bridgeless river with great difficulty and went to Maumee City on the other side. There I found two or three Catholics, said mass for them and set out for Toledo."

"Toledo was then (1839) a real *mudhole*, on the banks of the Maumee. It consisted of a few frame houses, some log cabins, an extent of swamp and an array of ponds of muddy water. A worse feature was that a large number of persons were sick with the Maumee fever. There were a few Catholic families and five or six single men. I said mass for eight or ten persons in the frame shanty of a poor Canadian." Father Machebeuf remained in Toledo a few days, hearing confessions and celebrating Mass in a room over a drugstore on an altar made up of dry-goods boxes covered with calico.

He then headed back up the Maumee River, visiting Catholics in the now ghost town of Providence, across from present-day Grand Rapids, before arriving in Napoleon. "The most of the Catholics living in this section were Irishmen, working on the [Miami and Erie] canal, chiefly near Napoleon. As they all lived in miserable tents, crowded and filthy, there was no corner for me among them." The father eventually secured quarters in the village tavern.

After a long day of visiting the camps of canal workers, Father Machebeuf returned to the tavern quite tired and looking forward to a quiet evening by a warm fire. Instead he found the tavern surrounded by horses and wagons and the building crowded with men. The tavern, being the largest building in town, also served as county court and a trial was underway. His room had been converted to a courtroom and, in the chair next to his bed, sat the judge.

Father Machebeuf took his supper elsewhere and returned to the tavern, determined to go to bed, trial or no trial. He pushed his way through the crowd, convinced three men sitting in his bed to move, drew the bed curtains shut and undressed and retired. "This situation caused a little merriment, but I did not mind that and was soon fast asleep." He awoke later to the sound of loud voices and heavy boots as court adjourned. "The prisoner came to my bed and asked me how I got along. I told him very well and asked him what was the decision of the court. He informed me that he got clear. He then left, and for the rest of the night I had a quiet and undisturbed sleep."

The father soon returned to Tiffin, where he spent most of the year of 1840. By early 1841 he had been transferred to Lower Sandusky, now Fremont, with the promise from his bishop in Cincinnati that he would be appointed pastor of the city of Sandusky once his English improved. Father Machebeuf looked forward to this move. "What has determined me to leave Lower Sandusky is that the town is built in a hollow on both sides of the river, and the atmosphere is not healthy in the summer. From August until October a good part of the inhabitants are down sick with the fever.

"Sandusky City, on the contrary, is extremely healthy the whole year, as it is built on the shore of Lake Erie which is like a little ocean. Its position is rather elevated and its soil gravelly, so that the air is never tainted with unhealthy exhalations and the wind, which has a clear sweep, keeps the atmosphere pure and wholesome."

By 1843, the father had received his Sandusky post and went about raising money to build churches, traveling as far as Montreal, Quebec, seeking funds. By 1846, Sandusky had three churches, including St. Mary's, which continues today. In late 1850, he accepted assignment to the American Southwest where over the years he would achieve near legendary status in New Mexico and in Colorado, where he was named first bishop of Denver—when he arrived in Denver, the city had one church and 35 saloons. He died in 1889 and his life and work in the Southwest drew the attention if not the fascination of the novelist Willa Cather who made him the subject of her 1925 novel, *Death Comes for the Archbishop*. Although she never met him she became intrigued as she learned of him through her travels in the Southwest. She wrote in a 1927 letter that she saw Father Machebeuf as "fearless and fine and very, very, well-bred. What I felt curious about was the daily life of such a man in a crude, frontier society."

Father Joseph Machebeuf as he appeared later in life. As a young priest he roamed the Great Black Swamp looking for Catholics to minister to.

This 1835 tavern in Napoleon also served as the first Henry County Courthouse. While staying as a guest there, Father Joseph Machebeuf's bedroom was turned into a temporary courtroom, a trial he slept through.

CHAPTER II

GLIMPSES OF NORTHWEST OHIO NATIVE AMERICANS

There is not a great deal of recorded history about the daily lives of the native inhabitants of northwest Ohio as they did not have written language and, for the most part, had been forced off their land and moved west before white settlers arrived in the area in any numbers. However there were some observations recorded by pioneers and settlers.

Wood County Ottawas

One early settler who was here and lived among the Native Americans was a man named Collister Haskins. Haskins was born in Massachusetts in 1799 and moved to what is now Waterville, Ohio, in 1818. In 1824 he bought land in Wood County, Ohio, south of what later became Bowling Green, and where he later laid out the village of Portage. He was considered to be the first interior settler of Wood County, his nearest white neighbor being 12 miles away. At the time there were four to five hundred Ottawa Indians living in the area and Haskins, before he died in 1872, recorded some observations of their daily lives. As there were goodly numbers of Ottawas living in Wood County until the latter 1830s, Haskins lived among them at least a dozen years, and traded with them regularly. The Ottawas were "kind neighbors and punctual to pay debts when trusted," according to Haskins.

"They subsisted mostly on flesh; they were fond of venison, turkeys, bear's meat and blue crane; they also ate porcupines, polecats, and musk rats. They were also fond of hominy which they obtained by pounding corn in a wooden mortar with a pestle attached to spring pole; they also made bean soup as a special luxury."

Spring found the Indians making maple sugar in large quantities. "As they had no other means of conveying it to market, they manufactured a kind of box made of elm bark about 18 inches in length, and 10 or 12 in width, and 16 or 18 in height. The bark was bent in proper shape and fastened with a thread of the same material. This was called a mowkon or mococks," according to Haskins. Each box held 50 to 100 pounds of sugar which were transported by horses, one box per side.

When sugar making was over, the Indians would pasture their horses on the fresh spring grass of area prairies and move on to the Maumee River valley to plant corn and beans. Summer was spent tending the crops and hunting and fishing, which continued into the fall when crops were gathered. In the winter, the Indians moved south of the Portage area into heavier woods, according to Haskins, "both on account of their own comfort and their horses, which subsisted in the winter on browse and the winter bunch grass, which is found only in the sheltered forest lands where the land is rather swampy; the Indian ponies would come out in the spring in good condition."

When it came to dress, the Ottawas made most of their clothes. "They dressed deer skins in the best manner. These they used for moccasins, leggings, mittens and shirts; and in cold weather they wore woolen blankets which they received as presents from the British Government. These were distributed at Malden, Canada West [now Amherstburg, Ontario] and were of excellent quality and very durable. During the warmer weather they might frequently be seen by the hundreds with no other clothing except the breech-clout, which consisted of two pieces of old blanket, or other old garment, about one foot square, one behind and the other before, strapped on about the hips and extending so far down as sufficed for decency. In this dress they were perfectly at ease in any company. The squaws being somewhat more particular, wore a skirt, generally of broadcloth, fastened at the waist, and extending below the knee."

When it came to jewelry and personal ornamentation, silver was very popular along with strings of beads woven into moccasins and incorporated into various parts of their dress. Bells were often fastened onto leggings so as to sound when walking and turkey feathers were displayed in the hair. "One old chief I have seen, wearing it was said, a thousand dollars worth of jewelry and ornaments and in the arrangement of these articles, it must be admitted, that they displayed considerable taste," Haskins observed.

Whiskey and tobacco were part of the Ottawa life, and death, as well. "When they buried one of their number they would pour whiskey upon the head of the grave; also tobacco was laid about the grave, which was always fenced with poles, built in the style of an old fashioned corncrib [and] covered with elm bark. A small aperture was left at the top, near the head of the grave, where you might generally see a plug of tobacco if the Indians were in the vicinity."

"When sickness visits the Indian's wigwam," according to Haskins, "they immediately resort to drumming and if the sickness is very severe, they drum night and day. In some respects the Indians excel as physicians, especially in midwifery, even extending their observations so far as to tell the sex of the unborn child an hour before its birth."

In addition to resident Ottawas, Haskins encountered many traveling Indians as well. "As I had located near or on the trail to Malden where some of the Indians received presents from the British, often hundreds of them camped round my house on their journey to and fro. They are almost universally harmless and friendly. The Wyandots and Sandusky Indians especially, often came into the vicinity."

Collister Haskins was witness to a moving religious ceremony when a large number of Wyandots camped near his house one September. The Wyandots were likely from a reservation that is now Upper Sandusky in Wyandot County. There was an active Methodist mission there where many of the Wyandots converted to Christianity. "It was a beautiful evening; the moon was full; the atmosphere was delightful; the sky was calm and clear. Hundreds of Indian ponies, each of them with its bell, were feeding near the camp.

"At about eight or nine o'clock we heard the voices of the Indians singing old 'Northfield.' When this ceased, the Indian preacher, or chief, led out in fervent prayer in the Indian language during which the most impressive silence prevailed in the camp. As he closed this petition all was silent again, except hundreds of bells, which rang harmoniously. Unexpected as this act of devotion was to us, it would be difficult to find words to express our feelings."

Ottawas in East Toledo

One of Toledo's pioneer citizens, Peter Navarre, recalled a large Ottawa village near the mouth of the Maumee River on its eastern bank, a story he related to an early *Toledo Blade* editor and historian, H. L. Hosmer. "At that time, 1807, the Indians of the Ottawa nation lived in a village on the Maumee, nearly opposite Manhattan [approximately where the Hungarian neighborhood of Birmingham is today]. It was a grassy plat; the houses of logs, about sixty in number, were built in two rows, whitewashed, and presented a cheerful and pleasant appearance. The village had been in existence since the days of Pontiac, and marked the site of his encampment on the Maumee at the time he left Detroit in 1764.

"At this time, also, the widow of Pontiac, Kantuckeegun, and his son, Otusso, dwelt at the mouth of the river. The old woman was held in great reverence, always the first one applied to by the nation for advice, and the first to sign all treaties. Otusso was a man of excellent sense, free from the vices of his tribe, and, with none of the ferocity, inherited all the bravery of his father. There were eight thousand of the Ottawas, at this time, living on the Maumee."

Peter Navarre described an annual religious ceremony and sacrifice conducted by the Ottawas. "Once a year they had a sacrifice of the best of everything they owned. On such occasions, which generally lasted three days, they would eat what they could, and burn the remnant of their food so that the dogs could not get it. About ten days before this annual sacrifice they would blacken their faces and eat and drink only in the afternoon. Thousands of them would assemble and erect a shanty where they held their feasts. They would make religious speeches and, with upraised hand, and by every outward demonstration, testify their reverence for the Great Spirit."

"At this time they drank but little liquor, were proud and vain, and many of them rich. Their robes were of fine cloths, bedizened with silver and gold coins, which jingled and glittered as they walked. Often chiefs would have several hundred dollars fastened to their dresses."

Native American Football

One of the earliest judges in the region of the Northwest Territory that later became Ohio, Jacob Burnet, made an annual journey in the late 1700s and early 1800s from Cincinnati to Detroit to attend to court matters on a course that took him through the Maumee Valley. Although he doesn't give an exact year, probably 1798 or 1799, he was witness to an Indian game of sport while at Blue Jacket's village in present-day Defiance.

On this journey, Burnet and his party arrived at the village on the Auglaize River about midday and accepted an invitation to remain there until the next morning. The Shawnee Chief Blue Jacket was away at the time, however the group was received very kindly by Delaware Chief Bukongehelas.

"In the course of the afternoon, he got up a game of football, for the amusement of his guests, in the true aboriginal style," Burnet wrote. "He selected two young men to get a purse of trinkets made up to be the reward of the successful party. That matter was soon accomplished and the whole village, male and female in their best attire, were on the lawn which was beautiful plain of four or five acres in the center of the village thickly set in blue grass. At each of the opposite extremes of this lawn two stakes were set up, about six feet apart."

It was to be a battle of the sexes and to even things out, the men could touch the ball with their feet only while the women could use both hands and feet and carry and throw ball as well. In order to dislodge the ball from the hands of a female player, the men could whirl her around or even throw her to the grass and kick it out of her hands. The two sides, about 100 on each, arranged themselves in the center of the lawn, the men on one side and the women on the other. The first team to drive the ball through the stakes of the other would be the winner.

"All things being ready the old chief came on the lawn and, saying something not understood by his guests, threw up the ball between the lines of the combatants and retired when the contest began," Burnet wrote. "The young squaws were the most active of the party and most frequently caught the ball; it was amusing to see the struggle between them and the young men which generally terminated in the prostration of the squaw on the grass before the ball could be forced from her hand.

"The contest continued about an hour, with great animation and with various prospects of success, but was finally decided in favor of the fair sex by the Herculean strength of a mammoth squaw who got the ball and held it in spite of the men to shake it from the grasp of her uplifted hand, till she approached the goal near enough to throw it through the stakes."

The women divided up their prize, a victory made even sweeter because it was accomplished in front of a distinguished audience which included Judge Burnet and Arthur St. Clair, Jr., attorney general for the Northwest Territory, and son of Arthur St. Clair, governor of the same. The group spent a pleasant evening and resumed their journey the next morning down the Maumee River and on to Detroit.

After completing their judicial duties there, they returned to the Maumee Valley some days later to present-day Waterville where they breakfasted with a man named Black Beard who one of their party knew, probably a local trader. He convinced them, for mysterious reasons, to cross the river at Roche de Bouef and continue their trip, Black Beard's son acting as a guide. That meant slogging through the Great Black Swamp or, "two days and a half of incessant toil and difficulty," according to Judge Burnet. They arrived back at the same Indian village on the Auglaize which they could have reached in about half the time had they stayed on the Maumee River trail.

But things had changed since their last visit. Blue Jacket, who had been away, had returned from Cincinnati with a large quantity of whiskey and there was quite a bit of drinking going on. A tipsy, elderly native woman greeted Attorney General

St. Clair with an amorous kiss and said, "You big man—Governor's son," and proceeded to flirt with him. And while the party was treated with kindness as they were before, they decided that, under the circumstances, they should press on, even though it was getting late in the day. This meant one more miserable and mostly sleepless night in the mosquito-infested Black Swamp. The following morning they reached the remains of Fort Adams, built by Anthony Wayne's army in 1794 on the St. Mary's River in present-day Mercer County. There they dined with the man and his native wife living there and continued home to Cincinnati.

Maumee Bay Deer Hunt

Some very early observations were made in the fall of 1757 by a man named James Smith, who was captured by Indians a couple of years earlier in Pennsylvania and adopted by the Caughnawaga tribe, Quebec Indians who had come south as allies of France during the French and Indian war. Smith was on a trading trip with several Indian families on the Canadian shore of Lake Erie when a council was held to decide whether to return south by hopping the Bass Islands or by sailing their canoes around Lake Erie's western shore.

The Bass Islands, Smith observed, "are but seldom visited; because early in the spring and late in the fall it is dangerous sailing in their bark canoes; and in summer they are so infested with various kinds of serpents (but chiefly rattlesnakes) that it is dangerous landing." He noted that the Wyandots and Ottawas hunted the islands, which were rich in raccoons, in the winter when the lake was frozen, and that it was not unusual for a single hunter to trap a thousand raccoons in a season. However when spring came the traps would be filled not with raccoons but with rattlesnakes emerging from hibernation. This led to "a received opinion among the Indians that the snakes and raccoons are transmutable; that a great many of the snakes turn raccoons every fall, and raccoons [into] snakes every spring."

The decision of the council was to sail around Lake Erie's western end and after two days, "we came to the mouth of Miami of the Lake [Maumee River] and landed at cedar point," near where Maumee Bay State Park is now. At that time it's unlikely there was single white settler in the entire Maumee Valley, save for a lone trapper or vagabond here and there.

There they had a communal deer hunt. The women and boys remained along the river and lakeshore while the men went inland and flushed deer toward the water. Soon "the squaws and boys were busy tomahawking the deer in the water and we shooting them down on land," Smith wrote. "We killed in all about thirty deer: tho a great many made their escape by water. We had now great feasting and rejoicing as we had plenty of homony, venison and wild fowl. . . . Here our company separated. The chief part of them went up the Miami River that empties into Lake Erie at cedar point whilst we proceeded on our journey."

Judge Jacob Burnet witnessed a game of Native American football in present-day Defiance around the year 1800.

CHAPTER III

FORT STARVATION AND A FATED MARCH TO FRENCHTOWN

It was early autumn 1812, and war was on again with England. An aging General James Winchester, the newly appointed commander of the Army of the Northwest, was leading troops from Fort Wayne down the Maumee River valley and things weren't going well at all. Winchester had replaced the popular William Henry Harrison and not only was he chronically short of supplies, his rough Kentucky volunteers were rebellious, disrespectful, and had taken a strong personal dislike of him. During the American Revolution more than three decades earlier, Winchester had performed gallantly and was a well-regarded figure. But this was another time and another war. Many of the newly recruited Kentuckians were younger men from the frontier; a hard-working, hard-drinking, independent lot used to doing what they wanted, when they wanted, and quite unaccustomed to directives such as:

Camp 28 miles from Fort Wayne Sept. 28th, 1812 General Orders
The attention of the officers is called to the several orders relative to the lines of March; and particularly to that of yesterday. The flank line must never depart so far to be beyond the sound of the drum of the centerline; nor the advanced guard so far from the pioneers, as to be beyond the sound of their axes. No noncommissioned officer or private shall struggle from the lines of march on any pretence what ever under the penalty of close confinement, for four days, and half Rations—The fortification around the encampment shall be in right lines and raised at least four feet high, and not nearer, and not nearer than 20 nor less than 15 feet in front of

the front line of troops. The brush to be cleared away on the outside of the fortification not less than thirty feet and the fires therein. Narrow spaces may be left in the breastwork, in front of each company, for the purposes of passing to and from the fires.

J. Winchester B. Genl.

Comdg. N.W. Army

Fort Winchester was built in on the Auglaize River near its confluence with the Maumee River in present-day Defiance in October 1812. From there an army led by General James Winchester went on a long and ultimately disastrous march to Frenchtown, now Monroe, Mich.

At one encampment along the way, perhaps the above camp, Winchester went to use his private commode at night and discovered, in an encounter of a personal and painful kind, that prankster soldiers had stretched a porcupine skin over it. It was definitely an omen of things to come.

Practical jokes aside, the morale of the soldiers was reaching crisis levels and appeals from Kentucky officials to the War Department led to a rapid reversal of the command decision. Winchester had left Fort Wayne on Sept. 23 and by Oct. 1 reached the confluence of the Maumee and Auglaize rivers and old Fort Defiance. The next day General William Henry Harrison arrived not only with a supply of flour but with the news that he had again been placed in command of the Northwestern Army, all to the lusty cheers and accompanying lift in morale of the men. Winchester's only crime may have been that he lacked the charisma and comparative youth of Harrison.

The old fort was in ruins and a new fort on the Auglaize River, which Harrison named Fort Winchester as sort of a consolation prize, was completed in only two weeks in what became a cold and rainy October. Winchester, now in command of the army's left wing, was to continue down the Maumee Valley to the rapids near the present-day city of Maumee, make camp, and await the arrival of two more wings of the army for an eventual wintertime attack on British-held Detroit and then on into Canada.

Fever spread through the men and daily burials became the norm and Winchester and his army of 1,000 plus left the fort Nov. 2 moving across to the north side of the Maumee River, hoping for dryer, higher land with more firewood and healthier conditions. The first two stops proved to be unsatisfactory and they finally settled on ground less than ten miles away between present-day Defiance and Napoleon, known officially as Camp Number 3. There the lack of supplies not only became critical but would bog them down for nearly two months. The private contractors on which the army depended for supplies were reluctant to make the difficult and, especially in wartime, dangerous journey to the Maumee Valley. Some making the attempt, as fall turned into winter, found their boats frozen in the ice of Maumee River tributaries.

Winchester's army began to really suffer. Most were still clad in summer-weight clothing, many had no boots and some literally had only rags wrapped around their feet. The chronic shortage of food led them to christen their encampment "Fort Starvation." Disease worsened through the camp as well, death was an almost daily occurrence, and some were sustaining themselves on boiled hickory roots. Discipline deteriorated as men wandered from camp in search of food, be it game, fish from the river, or wild nuts and berries. Courts martial for various offenses were common.

On Dec. 16, the men had not been issued a ration of flour for six days and were near mutiny. The next day a contractor with 300 hogs arrived and in the following days supplies began to arrive with a bit more regularity, clothing from home included.

On Christmas Eve, a Kentucky volunteer named Elias Darnell wrote, "Our sufferings at this place have been greater than if we had been in a severe battle. More than one hundred lives have been lost owing to our bad accommodations! The sufferings of about three hundred sick at this time, which are exposed to the cold ground, and deprived of every nourishment are sufficient proofs of our wretched condition! The camp has become a loathsome place." (The location of Camp Number 3, or "Fort Starvation," is placed by one historical account in Sections 22 and 23, Richland Township, Defiance County, which today is rolling forest and farmland overlooking State Route 424 and Independence Dam State Park. The over 100 soldiers that died there were buried in unmarked graves near the bank of the Maumee River.)

On Dec. 30 the army finally began to move down the Maumee River again which moved Darnell to a bit of sarcasm. "After nearly three months preparation for this expedition we commenced our march in great splendor; our elegant equipage cast a brilliant lustre on the surrounding objects as we passed! Our clothes and blankets looked as if they never had been acquainted with water, but intimately with dirt, smoke and soot."

The soldiers pulled the supply sleds themselves for the most part, given there were only a few packhorses and those quite undernourished. They endured a thaw that turned the snow to mud, then a very heavy snowfall, followed by a deep freeze. Camp was made at night by clearing away deep snow, trying to stay warm by smoky fires made from wet wood, and sleeping on the ground. Several days into the downriver march, Winchester received a letter from Harrison advising, but not ordering him, to turn back but he continued on.

They reached the Maumee Rapids and Roche de Bouef on Jan. 9 and on the next day made camp at Presque Isle Hill, a high plain along what is now River Road between present-day Waterville and Maumee city. Elias Darnell observed, "This place has a solemn appearance. The inhabitants have fled, and the Indians or British have burned their houses leaving some of the chimneys standing. By every appearance, this has been a respectable settlement." The settlers that fled left behind several hundred acres of corn which eased the supply shortage some. The soldiers were soon pounding the corn into meal and making bread.

While at the encampment at Presque Isle Hill, messengers from Frenchtown on the River Raisin (now Monroe, Michigan) brought news that the British and their Indian allies had been harassing the village there, seizing supplies, and threatening to burn it down. Life had become very uncertain for Frenchtown residents ever since Detroit, only about 30 miles north, had fallen to the British the previous August. More Frenchtown settlers arrived expressing fears that the village would be destroyed and asking Winchester for protection. On the evening of Jan. 16, General Winchester called a meeting of his senior officers and the majority were in favor of sending a strong detachment there. Frenchtown was reported to be lightly guarded and, temptingly, to have ample provisions. The next morning the general dispatched two detachments of about 675 soldiers under the command of Colonel Lewis, Darnell included, which was a violation of Harrison's orders for the army to remain at the Maumee Rapids until all units arrived.

They traveled down the frozen Maumee River to the shore of Maumee Bay where they spent the night in a French village, also known as Presque Isle. The sight of this simple village filled the men with "cheerfulness & joy," according to Darnell, it being the first bit of civilization seen after nearly five months of misery in the wilderness. Trekking along the frozen shore of Lake Erie the next day they neared Frenchtown, which was located on the north side of the River Raisin, in the early afternoon on the 18th. The British had only about 100 combined regulars and Canadian militia soldiers backed up by about 200 Indians and a single cannon. Assisting the Americans were about 100 French civilians of the settlement. The British and Indians put up a brief resistance, then went into an orderly retreat north, using the cannon for cover fire.

The Americans lost 12 killed and 55 wounded, many in fruitless pursuit of the British and Indians into the forest beyond the village limits. "It would have been better for us if we had been contended with the possession of the village without pursuing them into the woods," Darnell wrote. Word of the victory was sent back to Winchester and the rest at Maumee Rapids, who were ecstatic at the news. The general quickly left for Frenchtown with about 250 additional troops, arriving there on the 20th. He then sent word back to Harrison apprising him of the situation and requesting additional reinforcements.

Although Winchester and his officers knew their position was vulnerable and fully expected a British counterattack, they didn't seem to attach all that much urgency to it. According to Elias Darnell on Jan. 21, "A Frenchman [Toledo pioneer citizen Peter Navarre according to other accounts] arrived here late in the evening from Malden [now Amherstburg, Ontario] and stated that a large number of Indians and British were coming on the ice with artillery to attack us; he judged their number to be 3,000; this was not believed by some of our leading men who were regaling themselves with whiskey and loaf sugar; but the generality of troops put great confidence in the Frenchman's report, and expected some fatal disaster to befall us." Although Navarre's estimate of 3,000 might have been twice the actual number, his disregarded intelligence report was otherwise entirely accurate. A second scout brought a similar report which was also discounted.

That night the Americans slept, spread out along the north side of the River Raisin with the left wing protected only by a

According to an old map, Winchester's army camped for nearly two months in the highlands near this creek above present-day State Route 424 in Defiance County in the fall and early winter of 1812. Bogged down by a lack of supplies, about 100 soldiers died of disease in a camp the soldiers dubbed "Fort Starvation."

picket fence, the right wing exposed in an open field, and with no extra guard posted or patrols sent out. Winchester slept in the comfortable home of Frenchtown resident Francois Navarre, Peter's father, over a half mile away and on the south side of the river. Meanwhile the British and Indians drew near, advancing to within an eighth of a mile undetected in early morning darkness of the 22nd.

At the first, faint light of a frozen predawn, an American sentry shot and killed a British soldier but it was all downhill from there. The British and Indians let loose with artillery and withering musket fire and, after about 20 minutes, the right wing retreated to the frozen river and attempted to regroup. From this point on, things collapsed completely and soon 400 American soldiers were running for their lives south, some throwing their weapons away, hotly pursued by Indians. Winchester and few other officers tried to rally the troops but they were surrounded on all sides. Before long some Indians were returning to Frenchtown with as many as eight or nine scalps hanging from their belts.

Winchester, along with his 17-year-old son, were captured by the Wyandot Chief Roundhead who seized his coat and hat and marched him shivering back to town. The action was still heavy there as the left wing, with the protection of the picket fence, was not only holding its own but had repelled the British advance three times, inflicting considerable losses in the process.

Winchester asked to see the ranking British officer, Colonel Henry Proctor, who demanded he surrender the rest. Winchester replied that he was no longer in command, as it had transferred to the senior officer on the left, but that he would recommend it.

A lull in the fighting around 10:00 a.m. brought forward a British flag of truce to those on the left who assumed that the British wanted a pause to collect their dead and wounded. "But how we were surprised and mortified when we heard that Gen. Winchester . . . had been taken prisoner by the Indians in attempting to rally the right wing," wrote Elias Darnell. The commander on the left agreed to surrender but only if Proctor consented to protect them from the Indians and care for the wounded. The British colonel agreed to post a guard and send sleds from Fort Malden for the wounded the next day.

If Proctor had any intentions of keeping his promises, that changed when he received a false report that William Henry Harrison was only eight miles away and advancing fast with a large force. The British had suffered substantial losses and were in no position to make a stand.

In what became known as The Battle of River Raisin, the Americans had lost around 200 dead or wounded while around 700 had been taken prisoner. Only 33 managed to escape the field and flee back toward Ohio. Meanwhile, Proctor and his troops hurried back toward Detroit, even leaving some of their own wounded, and those American prisoners who could walk went with them. The nonambulatory wounded were taken into homes and cabins of the town, protected by a token British guard. Elias Darnell was not wounded but stayed behind to tend to those who were, including his brother Allen. There were 30 wounded in the house he was in.

They spent a long night of dread and in the morning their worst fears were realized when about 200 Indian warriors, faces painted black and red, returned to Frenchtown. Soon, a general massacre was underway; some of the wounded were dragged outside and stripped, shot or tomahawked, and scalped while others died when the buildings they were in were set afire, unable to move and screaming for help. "My feeble powers cannot describe the dismal scenes here exhibited," Darnell wrote. Around 60 Americans were killed, their naked, bleeding bodies left to freeze in the January snows, the Indians warning the few remaining Frenchtown residents they weren't to dare to attempt to bury any of their hated enemy. The event became known as the River Raisin Massacre.

The rest were marched back toward Detroit, and those wounded who could not keep up were killed along the way, a fate suffered by Allen Darnell. Elias survived and was taken by an Indian family for a planned adoption. However he quickly escaped and joined the other prisoners at Fort Malden, the majority of whom were paroled in February and returned to Kentucky.

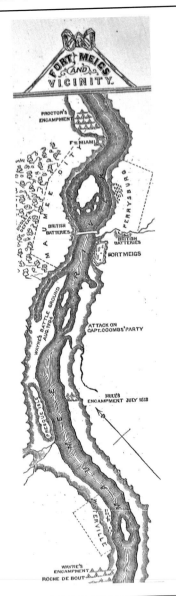

A map published by War of 1812 historian Benson Lossing in 1868 shows the location of various Maumee Valley historical sites including Presque Isle Hill, the last river camp of Winchester's army.

Word of events at Frenchtown spread throughout the country which intensified anti-British feelings and led calls for a renewed war effort. Many British were disturbed as well, as a Malden doctor wrote: "Be assured we have not heard the last of this shameful transaction. I wish to God it could be contradicted." Indeed, the following October when the British and Indians were defeated at The Battle of Thames in Ontario which ended the War of 1812 in the Northwest Theater, the rallying cry, "Remember the Raisin" came from the throat of every Kentucky soldier.

What Was Winchester Thinking?

In the aftermath of the River Raisin debacle, General James Winchester was, not surprisingly, criticized on several fronts: for failing to reverse his march down the Maumee River when so advised; for leaving the Maumee Rapids against orders; and for failing to better secure Frenchtown after the initial success there.

In his defense, the movement down the Maumee after nearly eight weeks at "Fort Starvation" created a boost in morale, which at that point had to be abysmal. Even though conditions were still very difficult, at least the soldiers were doing *something* instead of sitting in the same miserable place, numbed by hunger, cold, and boredom day after day. That he didn't want to ask them to go back is understandable.

His decision to send troops from Maumee Rapids to Frenchtown, then go there himself, was influenced by several factors. He understood it to be lightly defended therefore it could be easily taken, which it was; the enlistment of his Kentucky volunteers would expire in February and most made it clear they would not reenlist, thus he would be soon losing most of his force; at Frenchtown there would be real food instead of frozen corn in the field and hickory tree roots, a powerful inducement; and he and his officers considered the protection of the residents there to be their soldier's duty.

After the war Winchester wrote that his move to Frenchtown was based, "on military principles as on those of humanity and political justice. And not to digress, the arms of the United States are as irrevocably bound to protect a single individual as a million. The social compact becomes a rope of sand, is rent asunder, the instant a single individual is sacrificed without his assent, even for the salvation of the republic."

There likely were personal motives as well as he had to be feeling deeply frustrated by that point. He had been leading an army for five months with absolutely nothing to show for it, had been demoted by those above him and treated with disrespect by those below, thus he may have seen the Frenchtown situation as a chance to prove himself.

His failure to better secure Frenchtown, given the proximity of British and Indian forces, and his dismissal of reports that they were en route the night before the defeat is puzzling to say the least. Canadian historian Pierre Berton, who wrote extensively about the War of 1812, suggested the euphoria following the initial victory coupled with the sudden presence of good food, whiskey, and real houses with beds and warm fires gave him a false, if not ethereal, confidence that blinded him. And when he received word the day before the fateful battle that Harrison and his force had reached the Maumee Rapids and would be there in 24 hours, he may have assumed he was out of the woods.

After he was taken prisoner Winchester was marched to Fort Malden where the next day he sent a letter to the U.S. Secretary of War apprising him of the defeat and noting, "However unfortunate may seem the affair of yesterday, I am flattered by a belief that no material error is chargeable upon myself . . ." Winchester was held prisoner for about a year then released.

Where Was Harrison?

General William Henry Harrison was camped at Upper Sandusky in present-day Wyandot County when he received the news on Jan. 18 from General Winchester that he was sending soldiers to the River Raisin, news that left him "astonished." Harrison's plans for an orderly gathering of all the troops at the Maumee Rapids now in disarray, he immediately dispatched units toward the Maumee from both Upper Sandusky and Sandusky.

The next day he hurried there himself to take command, arriving at the Presque Isle Hill outpost on the 20th and probably was again astonished to find both Winchester and most of his men also gone. He ordered the newly arriving units to march to the River Raisin with all due speed, and made plans to go there himself. On the frozen morning of the 22nd he wrote the governor of Kentucky that, "All will be well if the post at the River Raisin can be maintained for a few days. . . ." But it was too late, the attack was already under way.

By 9:00 a.m. that morning, the first of those who had fled from the battle reached the forward American relief units marching along Lake Erie, word that reached Harrison about noon. By mid-afternoon both Harrison and a total of 900 men were rushing north but the reports from both fleeing survivors and Frenchtown citizens painted a bleak picture. By dark, the march was halted and the next morning a retreat began. Harrison was in a difficult situation as he had lost a significant portion of his army and had no way of knowing if British and Indian forces were headed for his position.

He and his officers briefly considered establishing themselves at Winchester's Presque Isle Hill camp at the Maumee Rapids. But it being on the opposite side from the supply lines on a river which, given the time of year, could go into flood at anytime, they decided against it. With no way to transport the supplies there, they set fire to the storehouses and everything else early on the 23rd and retreated to the Portage River, also known then as the Carrying River, in present-day Pemberville to regroup.

On the 24th, Harrison wrote Ohio Governor Return Jonathan Meigs: "Headquarters, Carrying River 24th Jan. 1813. Dear Sir, The event of which I expressed so much apprehension in my letter to you from Lower Sandusky has happened. . . . Never were the affairs of any army in a more prosperous situation than ours before the unfortunate step of marching the detachment to the river Raisin; it was made not only without any authority from me but in opposition to my views. . . . Unless the weather is very unfavorable, I shall be at the Rapids again in four or five days and shall certainly give the enemy the opportunity of measuring their strength with us in another contest. For myself I feel no doubt as to the result, and if I can judge of the disposition of the troops, from the manner in which they received an address from me yesterday, a desire of avenging their lost comrades and retrieving their country's disgrace is the predominant passion that occupies their minds."

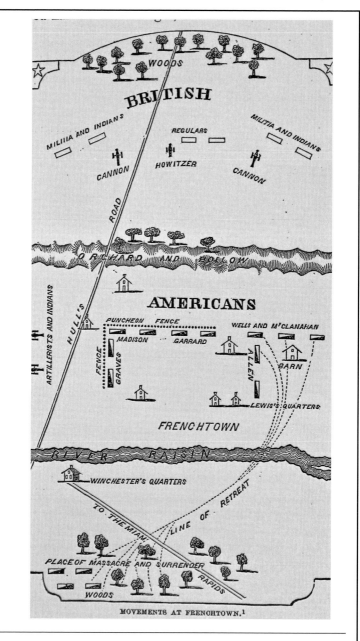

Map of the battle positions and line of American retreat during The

Battle of River Raisin in January 1813.

CHAPTER IV

FORCED MARCH ACROSS THE BLACK SWAMP

January 24, 1813

It was just past midnight in present-day Upper Sandusky and a wet snow weighed down the wind-whipped tents of sleeping soldiers left behind by William Henry Harrison when a call to arms broke their slumber. Their orders were to leave immediately to join the general who had broken off his march to Frenchtown and was withdrawing to the Portage River.

By about 3:00 a.m., the march began into the dark and dismal January night, a trek that would take them on a course through the heart of the Black Swamp. They left their tents and camp equipment behind, taking knapsacks and blankets. Had it been colder and the swamp been frozen solid, it might have been a fairly unremarkable journey. Harrison, in fact, had been planning a winter invasion of Canada, counting on the Black Swamp and area rivers and grounds to be frozen. However a January thaw typical of northwest Ohio winters was in place.

One of the soldiers making the march was Alfred Lorrain, from the Petersburg (Virginia) Volunteers, who later wrote of his experiences. An experienced guide led the detachment which marched in single file, it being so dark that each kept in physical contact with his predecessor to keep from getting lost. "We plunged and floundered through brush and brier, deep creeks and rising waters, mingled with drift and ragged fragments of ice. We longed for the day, but when light broke upon us it seemed to augment our wretchedness by calling into painful exercise an additional sense, and greatly enlarging the scene of desolation." To make things worse it began to rain.

They regularly had to cross standing ponds of water, following a trail of shattered ice made by preceding soldiers and horses. "While fording such places our feet would get so benumbed that we seemed to be walking on bundles of rags and it was really a luxury to come to a parenthesis of mud and mire, for then we could feel a returning glow of vitality. Occasionally a poor packhorse would fall down in his track—if tracks there were—to rise no more forever. It was heartrending to see them roll their flashing eyes indignantly on the passing soldiers, as though to rebuke the madness of the people in driving to such an extremity of suffering. Droves of hogs, which had been abandoned to the wilds, grim, gaunt, and hungry as the grave, were squealing through the woods, and rooting up the snow; and under the relentless scourge of war the whole creation seemed to groan in pain," Lorrain wrote.

"We passed by one of our subaltern officers, who was trembling like an aspen, and beseeching every soldier for a dram, declaring that he would perish in a few minutes if not supplied. Poor fellow! He had been in the habit of keeping himself always under the influence of liquor, and his supply had failed him in this day of affliction. By draining several canteens, he obtained enough to drag him through the horrors of the day."

The soldiers' morale received a boost when they neared Hull's Trace, a track hacked through the wilderness the previous summer by General Hull's expedition on its way to Detroit. "It is true we had never heard it spoken of by those who had seen it except in terms of unqualified execration [cursing], but still it was a road, and there was a kind of redeeming sound in the phrase that struck pleasantly on the drum of the ear. . . . But O! the burst of indignation that followed . . . there had evidently been an opening made through the dense forest but the road, if there had ever been any, had been mostly washed away before our time." Hull's group had felled trees and laid a corduroy road in places, but the logs had been floated and cast about by the high water, creating even more of an impediment than might have otherwise existed.

Despite the conditions, they managed to make fairly good progress by the time the January darkness began to return. Another member of the Petersburg Volunteers wrote, "That day I regretted being a soldier. On that day we marched 30 miles under an incessant rain. . . . In this swamp you lose sight of terra firma altogether—the water was about 6 inches deep on the ice, which was very rotten, often breaking through to the depth of four or five feet."

They found some reasonably high ground, scraped away the snow, built fires, and spread their blankets and lay down. "How long we lay that night in a shivering condition before we fell asleep we could never ascertain; but I awoke in the morning from pleasant dreams and in a profuse perspiration and, as I thought, under a heavy press of blankets; but when I threw up my arm to take an observation and to see how the land lay, an avalanche of virgin snow, which had silently ministered to my comfort during the night, tumbled into my bosom and quickly aroused me to a recollection of my proper latitudes and true bearings and I found, by calculation, that I was bounded north, south, east, and west by the Black Swamp," Alfred Lorrain wrote. The rain had changed to snow overnight, covering everyone with about five inches.

However the bulk of the journey was over and the Portage River encampment was soon reached. "As we marched in every man was presented with a small glass of high wine. When I drank my allowance, it produced an indescribable titillation reaching to the ends of my toes and fingers." Here they also received rations, however scant, and settled down for the night only to again be awakened at midnight, this time by the shouting and firing of sentries and the call to arms by officers. It seemed "that all the northern tribes were charging upon us, front, flank and rear." That is until an old army veteran came along, snickering, "Boys, did you never hear the wolves howl before?"

It wasn't until Jan. 30 that all the Upper Sandusky troops and artillery, as well as some from Lower Sandusky (Fremont), were able to reach the Portage River. Early on Feb. 1, with falling temperatures refreezing the mud, General Harrison and his army marched back to the north, leaving before many had a chance to eat breakfast. They reached the Maumee River the following morning, which, frozen solid, provided the weary group smooth avenue for traveling. As they made their way downriver, the hungry force came across a bottomland of Indian corn that had not been harvested. "As soon as we entered this inviting field the army broke in every direction like a drove of frightened cattle," Alfred Lorrain wrote. "Deaf to the commands of our officers, and regardless of all military order, we tore down the precious ears and filled our pockets and bosoms till we were richly laden with the spoils of the field. With the musket in one hand, and an ear of corn in the other, we marched on greedily devouring the unstinted supply of a merciful Providence. . . . We were amazed that we had lived so long in the world and had never discovered the transcendent luxury of raw corn."

Later that day, they arrived at the foot of the rapids of the Maumee between the present-day cities of Maumee and Perrysburg where William Henry Harrison ascended the high south bank. He saw the strategic advantage of the location and, with hopes of a wintertime invasion of Canada all but over, ordered the building of a garrison which he could not have known would come to be a permanent part of the northwest Ohio historical scene, Fort Meigs.

The chaos that followed the American defeat at The Battle of River Raisin led retreating soldiers to meet reinforcements and reorganize at what is now William Henry Harrison Park in Pemberville.

CHAPTER V

THE BATTLE OF LAKE ERIE

September 10, 1813

Dawn on a pleasant September morning at Put-in-Bay on South Bass Island found the sun lighting the eastern skies as gulls swooped and called about the picturesque harbor and around the masts of American warships anchored there. But then the tall masts and sails of British warships sprouted on the horizon and the only sea battle ever to be fought on the waters of Lake Erie was about to begin. Commander of the American fleet, Commodore Oliver Hazard Perry, 28, had been stationed on the eastern seaboard when the war started and, after seeing little action, requested and received a transfer to the Great Lakes the previous February.

Perry's fleet, two large brigs christened the Lawrence *and the* Niagara, *and seven smaller ships, had sailed to Put-in-Bay less than a month earlier after being hastily built at Erie, Penn., and about 40 percent of his 500-plus man crew were actually soldiers as opposed to sailors. But the fleet's presence in the western Lake Erie basin had cut off the water supply route to the British Fort Malden and posts beyond. Perry and his nine-ship flotilla had been expecting the British and were soon sailing out to meet them.*

The British fleet also featured two large ships, the Detroit *and the* Queen Charlotte, *along with four smaller ones, and it would be the four large ships of the two fleets that would drive the battle's outcome. The British were commanded by a more experienced Robert*

Barclay, also 28, who had served over half his life in the Royal Navy, had fought at the Battle of Trafalgar off the coast of Spain in 1805, one of the epic sea clashes in history, and who later lost an arm in action in 1808.

Although the British had three fewer ships, they had more total cannons including more long-range guns. To negate this and to take advantage of his more numerous but short distance carronades (a recently invented cannon that could be loaded and fired faster, required less gunpowder and gun crew, and fired a much heavier ball than a long gun), Commodore Perry sailed within close range and by around noon commenced a bloody, three-hour slugfest. Naval battles fought at close range in wooden ships were particularly brutal, more so than land battles. Not only were sailors concentrated in a small area with nowhere to run from the variety of iron shells and shot that were fired, but cannonballs smashing into a ship produced a tremendous amount of wood shrapnel, ranging from slivers to jagged planks. Two who were at this naval battle and later wrote about it were Surgeon's Mate Usher Parsons and Seaman David G. Bunnell, a gunner, both of whom were aboard Perry's flagship the Lawrence.

David G. Bunnell

As the American fleet sailed out, Commodore Perry unfurled his battle flag, a blue and white banner which the men had not seen before, its words, "Don't Give up the Ship" led to three cheers. The words were the dying declaration of a close friend, Captain James Lawrence, who had been mortally wounded in an Atlantic sea battle earlier in the summer and for whom Perry had named his ship.

With light winds, the fleet approached the British line slowly, which gave David Bunnell and his fellow sailors time for reflection. "The word 'silence' was given—we stood in awful impatience—not a word was spoken—not a sound heard, except now and then an order to trim a sail and the boatswain's shrill whistle. It seemed like the awful silence that precedes an earthquake. . . . All nature seemed wrapped in awful suspense—the dart of death hung as if trembling by a single hair, and no one knew on whose head it would fall."

The silence ended about 11:45 a.m. when musicians aboard the British flagship *Detroit* played "Rule Britannia" and the ship fired a ranging shot at the *Lawrence* which missed. A second shot a few minutes later smashed into the ship's starboard side killing and wounding American sailors, and the battle was on. Perry continued his advance, his ships absorbing punishment from British long-range guns and by about 12:15 they had closed to within carronade range and began firing broadsides. The battle was now fully underway and the cannons' roar thundered across Lake Erie and was heard on the Ontario, Michigan, and Ohio shores.

The *Lawrence* was raked by withering gunfire and "my comrades fell all around me," Bunnell wrote. A man standing next to him had both legs blown off and soon five of his eight-man gun crew were either dead or seriously wounded. "At last my gun got so warm it jumped entirely out of its carriage, which rendered it useless. I went to the next gun and found there was but one man left, but with the assistance of my three was soon made to play again." One horribly injured sailor laid on the deck, begging Commodore Perry to put him out of his misery, something Perry could not bring himself to do. The man died about an hour later. At one point in the battle, another man's brains flew into David Bunnell's face and "I was for some time blinded, and for a few moments was at a loss to ascertain whether it was him or me that was killed."

For two grueling hours, the *Lawrence* slugged it out essentially alone with the *Detroit* and *Queen Charlotte* as her sister ship, the *Niagara*, held back, essentially out of fighting range. One by one the guns of the *Lawrence* fell silent. With a casualty rate approaching 80 percent, there was no one left to fire them. "The deck was in a shocking predicament," Bunnell wrote. "Death had been very busy. It was one continued gore of blood and carnage—the dead and dying were strewed in every direction over it—for it was impossible to take the wounded below as fast as they fell." It was now approaching 2:30 p.m. and the ship was a battered wreck, its sails ragged strips, its pockmarked and blood soaked deck strewn with bodies, debris, and disabled artillery.

With only ten men left standing out of nearly 100, Perry's options were to surrender or try to make it to the *Niagara.* Choosing the latter, he gave the order "man the boat," lowered his flag and left in a rowboat. The *Niagara* at this point in the battle was practically unscathed, much to Perry's surprise and dismay, leaving the *Lawrence* to take the brunt of British fire (this was the topic of a later and bitter dispute between Perry and the ship's commander who argued that his orders were unclear.) Despite the waters erupting around the rowboat from continuous British fire, the frantically rowing four-man crew and the commodore made it to the *Niagara,* soaked but unharmed. (From this point David Bunnell describes the action on the *Niagara* although he doesn't specifically state that he accompanied Perry on the rowboat over.)

Once aboard, Perry resumed command and with a fresh ship and its carronades to bring to bear, he continued to pound the British fleet. "The only words I recollect hearing Perry say were—'take good aim boys, don't waste your shot,'" Bunnell wrote. He observed the toll the battle was taking on animals as well: a pig loose on deck feeding on spilled peas, despite having both hind legs blown off; and a small dog, pet to one of the officers, had been injured and ran about yelping in pain and terror. Adding to the hellish scene was smoke so thick "that it was impossible to see the enemy—but we were so close to them that by firing on a level we could not miss."

Now about three hours into the battle, a bit of luck came the Americans way as the battered *Detroit* had collided with its sister ship *Queen Charlotte* and their riggings had become entangled. Commodore Perry sailed directly toward the British line and breached it. With three British ships to starboard and three to port, Perry unleashed deadly carronade volleys from both sides of the *Niagara* while some of the smaller American ships joined in. Fighting from a range of less than 50 yards, Perry continued to hammer both ships which, despite their predicament still managed to return fire, felling over 20 *Niagara* crew members.

British sailors feverishly hacked away at the tangled riggings and managed to get the two heavily damaged ships separated but by then to fight any more was pointless. The *Queen Charlotte* lowered her colors followed by the *Detroit* and the other four British ships soon followed suit. As was the case with the *Lawrence*, "the English Commander's ship *Detroit* looked like a slaughterhouse," Bunnell noted. And Commander Robert Barclay lay below deck having been wounded twice, his second one serious and disabling his remaining arm.

"What a glorious day to my country," Bunnell wrote, "and how rejoiced was I to find the battle ended—victory on our own, and myself safe, except a slight wound and much deafened. I did not recover my proper hearing for a year afterwards."

Usher Parsons

While the Battle of Lake Erie raged, Surgeon's Mate Usher Parsons waged a different battle aboard the *Lawrence*, trying to keep up with the steady stream of casualties. Working alone because the surgeon was sick with fever, Parsons had six men to help carry the wounded and restrain them during "surgery" which consisted of sewing wounds shut or applying tourniquets to those bleeding badly, splinting fractured bones, and performing amputations only if the limb was dangling, saving the others for later when there was more time. Physical restraint was needed in the absence of anesthesia.

In a typical ship of war, the wounded would be brought to a room well below deck for safe haven and treatment. However the shallow-drafted *Lawrence* provided no such luxury and rooms at water level had to be used. Parsons had to contend with both scores of wounded and an occasional cannonball crashing through the side of the ship into the area he was working. One wounded sailor was killed by a shell literally while Parsons' hand rested on him.

"An hour's engagement had so far swept the deck," Parsons recalled, "that new appeals for surgical aid were less frequent; a remission at this time very desirable both to the wounded and myself; for the repeated request of the Commodore to spare him another man had taken from me the last one."

Parsons described the reaction of the wounded when Commodore Perry was forced to lower the flag and abandon the *Lawrence* for the *Niagara*. "The effect of this on the wounded was distressing in the extreme; medical aid was rejected and little else could be heard from them than 'sink the ship—let us all sink together.'" But this state of despair was short-lived as the victory over the British once Perry reached the *Niagara* "changed the horrors of defeat into shouts of victory. . . . The action terminated shortly after three o'clock and, of about one hundred men reported fit for duty in the morning, twenty-one were found dead and sixty-three wounded."

With the battle over, it now fell to Usher Parsons to oversee the recovery of the wounded over the following weeks, a goodly number of whom did recover. Parsons attributed this to the purity of the air both aboard the ships then later ashore; the substantial quantity of fresh meats, vegetables, and dairy products provided to the men by grateful Ohio farmers after the battle, and by the positive state of mind that being on the victorious side produces. Parsons came away convinced "that this state of mind has a greater effect than has generally been supposed; and that the surgeon on the conquering side will always be more successful than the one who has charge of the vanquished crew."

As the last smoke of battle drifted over the once-again quiet waters of Lake Erie, Commodore Perry scribbled his now legendary message to General William Henry Harrison: "We have met the enemy and they are ours: Two Ships, two Brigs, one Schooner & one Sloop." That evening American and British sailors bowed their heads together as dead from both sides were buried at sea. And when the battered fleets returned to Put-in-Bay, six dead officers, three British and three American, were buried side by side on South Bass Island, the badly wounded Commander Barclay leaning against Commodore Perry for support during the service.

The defeat of the British fleet gave the Americans full control of Lake Erie and the way to Canada lay open. In less than a month, the British were defeated at the Battle of Thames and war would never again visit the region. After the war Usher Parsons continued in the naval service and earned a medical degree from Harvard. In 1822, he married the sister of the poet Oliver Wendell Holmes and later served as a professor of anatomy and surgery at Brown University and as president of the Rhode Island Medical Society. David Bunnell also continued in the naval service, was captured on Lake Huron in

1814, and was imprisoned in England briefly before returning home. He published his memoir in 1831.

Author's note: Other stories regarding the War of 1812 in northwest Ohio appear in both *The Great Black Swamp* and *The Great Black Swamp II*.

This wall mural above the west entrance of the Ottawa County Court-house in Port Clinton portrays Commodore Oliver Hazard Perry trans-ferring his flag at the height of the Battle of Lake Erie. While the mural is somewhat dramatized in its detail, Perry did stand for part of the journey to another ship until the sailors rowing insisted he sit down.

CHAPTER VI

The Marshes of Lake Erie, 1813

Samuel R. Brown was a green soldier stationed at Fort Meigs in 1813 when he was sent with four others to the Portage River to deliver a communication to another post. The route they took was to travel down the Maumee River then east along the Lake Erie shore. For Brown it was a journey fraught with fear as it was his first foray beyond the protection of the fort, traveling through hostile territory with only a small party. However that did not stop him from making some observations of the Lake Erie marshes through which they attempted to travel, or as he called them, the "Great Meadow." The virgin marshes were then the northern perimeter of the Great Black Swamp and are now the Swamp's largest intact remnants.

"The Great Meadow cannot contain less than two hundred thousand acres," Samuel Brown wrote. "Its bank is generally about eight feet above the surface of the lake. The soil is sufficiently dry for ploughing and traces of old Indian corn hills are frequently met with. I had the best opportunity for exploring that part which lies between Miami bay [Maumee Bay] and Portage river.

"We descended the Miami [Maumee River] in a canoe and at sun set had just reached the bay which, like that of Sandusky, has every appearance of a lake." They then traveled several miles east along the lakeshore, making camp about midnight. Brown's colleagues, who were experienced at these types of conditions, slept soundly while he never closed his eyes, jumping at every sound. A storm whipped up the moody waters of Lake Erie and morning found their canoe swamped, their provisions and ammunition soaked. "Here we were; in an Indian country with nothing to defend ourselves with but an ax and a musket which could not be discharged."

From there they attempted to save some miles by angling inland through what today is the Cedar Point Wildlife Refuge. As difficult as the head-high grass made travel, it was the appearance of rattlesnakes that convinced them to return to the lakeshore, particularly since one in their party was barefoot. They proceeded on foot along the lake, reaching the wide waters of the Toussaint River about midday. With one of the members of the group being unable to swim, and no wood around to make a raft, they again tried to go inland through what is now part of the Ottawa National Wildlife Refuge, hoping to find woods.

They made it about two miles before giving up and retreating back to the lakeshore. They then backtracked along the shore about a mile and tried again. "It is impossible for me to give the reader a perfect idea of the difficulties and fatigue we experienced in getting to the grove," Brown wrote. "The grass was about 7 feet high and so thick that it would easily sustain one's hat—in some places a cat could have walked on its surface; in many places it was effectually matted by vines that required one's whole strength to break down." They were only able to clear "four rods" at a time, or about 22 yards, before resting.

By nightfall they reached a wooded grove on a branch of the Toussaint and "wet, fatigued and supperless, we lay down on the moist ground and had but two blankets among the five of us. Not a moments sleep for my eyes this night; but neither the danger of the rattlesnake's fangs or the horror of the scalping knife had any influence with my comrades; they slept as soundly as though they had been under their paternal roofs. But they had been so long familiarized to danger, that it had lost its terrors—*I was a raw hand*; hence the difference. The geese, ducks, and other fowl kept up an incessant noise the whole night. The dew had the effect of a shower—our clothes and blankets were as wet as though they had been exposed to a heavy rain."

The next morning they resumed their marshy march, but by mid-morning were exhausted and returned to the Lake Erie shore and the mouth of the Toussaint, preferring to deal with the dangers of a river crossing. There, they had a bit of luck as they found a large piece of driftwood to raft over both their clothes and the man who could not swim, some fresh tracks made by Indians and their horses making all a bit nervous. There Brown continued his observations. "It is no exaggeration to say we met with rattle snakes every ten rods from the Tous Saints to Portage river. The grass of this meadow is of a softer kind than the wild grass of the prairies and answers all the purposes of hay and pasture. It is intermixed with wild oats, wild rye, wild peas, beans &c, [etc.] making it in short, the best range for cattle or horses I ever saw."

"The Tous Saints is an unfrequented solitary river, and the best place for fowling this side of Detroit. To those attached to this kind of sport, it is worth a journey of five hundred miles to view the feathered assemblage which almost covers the surface of the river and sometimes darkens the air with their numbers."

Samuel Brown was similarly impressed with the waterfowl and natural food supply he saw on Maumee Bay. "Within the boundary of this bay grow several thousands acres of folle avoine, [wild oats] which constitute the principal food of the vast flock of ducks that frequent the place. It grows in about 7 feet in the water; the stalks near the roots are about an inch in diameter and grow to a height of about ten feet; its leaves above the surface of the water are like those of the reed cane; in other respects it resembles the common oat stalk in every thing but size and kernel, which is the nature of rice and of which the French people make free use in their favorite soup. Its yield is very abundant, being half a pint at least from every stalk."

Samuel Brown went on to note that he had observed this aquatic grain at the mouths of all Lake Erie tributaries west of the city of Sandusky as well as those at the south end of Lake Michigan. He described how ducks harvested the grain from the upper reaches of these ten-foot stalks. "She presses her breast against the stalk and with a violent effort of her feet causes it to yield to her strength, which it readily does by reason of its slender fibrous roots—having forced the top of the stalk into the water, she keeps it under her body until she has finished her repast."

The observant Brown also noted the protective barrier beach of Lake Erie that ran the length of the marshes as well as older, inland beaches. "If I were disposed to indulge in geological speculations on the formation of this vast plain, I would contend that lake Erie was, in former ages, several miles wider than at present, and I would prove my argument by the state of the second bank at the woods, where are to be found cylindrical or water worn stones, muscle shells, hillocks of sand [and] other evidences of the action of this inland sea."

After the war, Samuel Brown returned east and wrote of his wartime experiences in *Views of the Campaign of the Northwestern Army* which was published in Burlington, Vermont, in 1814. He died in 1817.

Samuel Brown made a dangerous journey across the marshes of Lake Erie in 1813. His party had difficulty crossing the Toussaint River, pictured above, where it empties into Lake Erie in what is now the Ottawa National Wildlife Refuge.

CHAPTER VII

THE GREAT RENEGADE

In the Maumee River between Napoleon and Defiance, the waters swirl around a peaceful atoll called Girty Island. Like so many locales in northwest Ohio, the atoll was named for an early pioneer who spent time in the area. When it comes to this individual's story, however, there is very little about it that was peaceful.

Of all the characters who roamed the ragged and often violent edge of civilization that was the Ohio frontier and northwest Ohio in the latter 1700s, probably none was so loathed and reviled by the settlers as the "great renegade," Simon Girty. Born to a pioneer family in central Pennsylvania, Girty would later in life fight against his countrymen for both the British and Indians in battles that shaped the destiny of the state of Ohio, earning a reputation for both treachery and extreme cruelty.

Many writers, both modern and historic including Theodore Roosevelt, have painted him in the darkest of hues: that of a torturing, scalping, murdering, traitor. He was the man who in 1782 stood and laughed when an American colonel, being slowly burned at the stake, begged him to take pity and shoot him. As late as 1968, an article about him in an historical magazine was titled, "A Wild Beast in Human Form."

Or was he? Where the man ends and the myth begins for this long-ago character is difficult to determine. What history generally agrees on is that Simon Girty was born in 1741 to Irish immigrant parents and violence was part of his upbringing. When he was about 10 his father was killed by an Indian in some sort of drunken dispute and at around age 15 he and his mother, brothers, and stepfather were captured by Indians when the frontier erupted in the French and Indian War. He and his family were forced to watch the burning of his stepfather at the stake. They then were scattered amongst several tribes, Simon ending up with the Senecas.

Girty spent three years in Indian captivity, ended officially by a 1759 treaty, although the exact time of his return to white society is not known. He is believed to have spent the next 15 years in and around Fort Pitt (Pittsburgh) where he became a trader and where his knowledge of both Indian ways and a number of languages made him very valuable as an interpreter. In 1774 he served Virginia in Dunmore's War, a conflict between that state and Ohio River Indians over white encroachment, and a year later when the American Revolution broke out, was loyal to the colonists' cause. However in 1778, he left Fort Pitt and made his way to Detroit where he gave his loyalty to the British who were allied with the Indians.

During the next five years until war's end, he served as liaison between the British and Indians and is believed to have personally led several Indian attacks on American soldiers, including Fort Laurens in eastern Ohio in 1779.

It was in June 1782 that an incident occurred that most vilified Girty in the minds of those on the Ohio frontier; the burning of Colonel William Crawford in present-day Wyandot County. Several months earlier, a different American colonel and his rogue militia had massacred and mutilated 96 peaceful Delaware Indian women, children, and older men, at a Moravian mission in Gnadenhutten. Crawford was captured by Delawares after a later battle and, even though he had no role in the massacre, was going to pay for it.

While the Indian burning of prisoners was not uncommon, suffice it to say that Crawford's was done slowly and designed to inflict the absolute maximum of agony. Simon Girty was present at the brutal affair and word of it spread like lightning through the Ohio country from two captured Americans who witnessed it but escaped. It was also reported that Girty was not only acquiescent to it but had, in fact, laughed at the horrifically suffering colonel. Girty's reputation was now that of monster, if it wasn't already.

The Revolution ended in 1783 but Girty continued to be active in Indian resistance to white settlement in western Ohio and his reputation grew still more. In the Ohio Indian Wars, he led the Wyandot contingent in the defeat of General Arthur St. Clair near present-day Fort Recovery in November 1791. With over 600 killed, it was the worst defeat ever of an American army. The following July, a young Indian captive named Oliver Spencer was taken to Shawnee Chief Blue Jacket's village on the Auglaize River in present-day Defiance. There he met Simon Girty.

Spencer's description of him, though written years later and probably embellished a bit, no doubt mirrored the sentiment of the time. He described Girty's "dark, shaggy hair, his low forehead; his brows contracted and meeting above his short, flat nose; his gray, sunken eyes averted the ingenuous gaze; his lips were thin and compressed, and the dark, sinister expression of his countenance to me seemed the very picture of a villain.

"He wore the Indian costume but without any ornament; and his silk handkerchief, while it supplied the place of a hat, hid an unsightly wound on his forehead. On each side in his belt was stuck a silver-mounted pistol and at his left hung a short, broad dirk, serving occasionally the uses of a knife. He made of me many inquiries; some about my family and the particulars of my captivity; but more of the strength of the different garrisons, the number of troops at Fort Washington [Cincinnati] and whether the President intended soon to send another army against the Indians. He spoke of the wrongs he had received at the hands of his countrymen and with fiendish exultation of the revenge he had taken.

"He boasted of his exploits, of the number of his victims, and of his personal prowess; then, raising his handkerchief and exhibiting the deep wound in his forehead (which I was after-wards told was inflicted by the tomahawk of the celebrated Indian chief Brant in a drunken frolic) said it was a saber cut which he had received in battle at St. Clair's defeat; adding with an oath that he had 'sent the damned Yankee officer' that gave it 'to hell.' He ended by telling me that I would never see home; but that if I should turn out to be a good hunter and a brave warrior I might one day be a chief."

While at Blue Jacket's village in 1792, Simon Girty was invited to a grand council that took place in October. It involved dozens of tribes from the Ohio frontier, Canada, and even from west of the Mississippi. Girty is believed to have been the only white person in attendance, such was his stature with area Indians.

In June, 1794 Girty participated in an attack on Anthony Wayne's troops at Fort Recovery, a newly built fort at the site of St. Clair's defeat three years earlier. This time things did not go well for the native side as they were repulsed with heavy losses. Two months later, Girty was in the field at the Battle of Fallen Timbers but kept his distance, perhaps knowing the day would end in disaster.

The defeat at Fallen Timbers and the resulting Treaty of Greenville a year later brought both the Ohio Indian Wars and Simon Girty's fighting days to an end, although his sinister reputation followed him to his grave and beyond. In later years, some historians have questioned the fairness and accuracy of this portrayal. In more recent years, so have some Girty descendants living in the Pittsburgh area questioned the reputation of their ancestor.

Just prior to his defecting in 1778, Girty accompanied a General Hand on an expedition to the Cuyahoga River to seize British ammunition believed to be hidden at an Indian village. Plagued by both poor weather and organization, Hand's group never reached their objective. His unruly militia instead attacked an Indian village that held only four women and a boy, killing all but one. The event became known derisively as the "Squaw Campaign," one Girty was said to have been disgusted to be associated with, and one that could have motivated him to alter his loyalty.

His behavior at the burning of the unfortunate Colonel Crawford in 1782 is, if nothing else, unverifiable. The event was carried out by Delaware Indians, with whom he had little influence, avenging the recent slaughter of fellow Delawares at Gnadenhutten. It's possible, if not probable, it didn't matter what Simon Girty or anyone else said; revenge was going to be had. The witnesses to the event who escaped were themselves awaiting the same fate, and presumably viewed the proceedings in a state of terror which could have affected their objectivity. According to another witness interviewed by noted Wisconsin historian Lyman Draper many years later, Girty did all he could to save Crawford, offering the Delawares his prize horse, rifle, and money, but to no avail.

In a separate but similar incident several years earlier, Girty is generally credited with saving the life of the famed frontiersman, Simon Kenton, who had been condemned to die. He is also credited with saving the lives of American captives who were condemned to be killed and with negotiating for release of others being held prisoner.

Two months after the Crawford incident, a combined British and Indian force attacked a fort at Bryan's Station in Kentucky. During that and the resulting Battle of Blue Licks, over 70 Americans were killed including both the legendary Daniel Boone's son and brother, with Daniel himself barely escaping. Word spread throughout the Ohio country that Simon Girty was the leader of the Indian forces in the battle, which was the bloodiest American defeat in the frontier theater of the Revolution. However, primary source reports on the clash, two British and two American, give Girty no leadership role at all, only that of an interpreter, placing leadership instead in the hands of a British captain. It seems that in the aftermath of the Crawford incident Girty had achieved the status of a super villain, capable of anything.

It's also interesting to compare the physical description of Girty by the Indian captive Oliver Spencer, given above, with that he gave of Chief Blue Jacket whom he met on the same day. In contrast to Girty, "the very picture of a villain," Blue Jacket was "finely proportioned, stout, and muscular; his eyes large, bright, and piercing; his forehead high and broad, his nose aquiline; his mouth rather wide and his countenance open and intelligent, expressive of firmness and decision." Yet as an ardent foe of white, westward expansion and a high ranking leader at St. Clair's bloody defeat less than a year earlier, Blue Jacket had more American blood on his hands than Simon Girty could possibly have had.

In the end, maybe it was Simon Girty switching sides during a war that doomed his reputation more than any of his actual deeds. He fought for not only one but two forces opposed to American interests, the British *and* the Indians. He left no spoken or written record of his motivation or his thinking in this matter. However he was known to be fond of the Indians and their way of life, having both lived with them for part of his adolescence and socialized and hunted with them as an adult. It's possible that during his three years at Fort Pitt he became aware of long-term American goals to conquer the native people and take their lands once the Revolution was over, plans he found to be morally unpalatable.

In the aftermath of Fallen Timbers and the transfer by treaty of Detroit to the United States in 1796, Girty spent his most of his remaining days on a farm in Malden, Ontario (now Amherstburg) near where the Detroit River and Lake Erie meet. He had been given a plot of land and a pension by the British for his service. He died in 1818, a frail and blind old man, and a detachment of British soldiers from Fort Malden fired a salute over his grave.

As for Girty Island, it is believed, but not certain, that Simon had a cabin on the north bank in present-day Henry County near the 40-acre island that bears the Girty name, about seven miles up the Maumee River from Napoleon. Legend has it that he would hide in the wild growth of the island whenever American soldiers were in the area as he constantly feared arrest and prosecution. What is more reliably known is that his brother James operated a trading post there. It's possible Simon merely stayed with James in his travels and never had his own residence, therefore the island drew its name from James.

The story of the island, like that of Simon Girty's life, is shrouded by the mists of time. He was a man who lived in two different worlds but left few footprints in either one.

Author's Note: In 2001, the Pennsylvania Historical and Museum Commission erected a Simon Girty marker in Dauphin County, Pennsylvania, near Harrisburg.

Frontiersman known as the "Great Renegade" was born nearby. Captured by Indians, 1756, he lived among the Senecas and learned their language and culture. Following his release, he became an interpreter for the American Army; deserted in 1778. Afterwards led British and Native American parties against frontier settlements. Hostile to the U.S. in the War of 1812, regarded as a loyalist by some and as a "white savage" by others, he remains controversial. He died in Canada.

Legend holds that the renegade Simon Girty would hide from American authorities in the wild growth of Girty Island in the Maumee River between present-day Napoleon and Defiance. The island remains covered with thick growth today.

CHAPTER VIII

NEITHER SNOW, NOR RAIN, NOR WOLVES

"Neither snow, nor rain, nor heat, nor gloom of night stays these couriers from the swift completion of their appointed rounds," is carved over the entrance to the Central Post Office building in New York City. Paraphrased from an actual quote by the fifth century B.C. Greek historian Herodotus, it serves as an unofficial motto for U.S. postal workers. The passage, however, does not come close to addressing a hazard faced by one early northwest Ohio mail carrier.

One of the earliest area mail carriers was a young teenager named John Butler of Fulton County who traveled a twice weekly route in the 1830s from Sylvania to LaGrange County, Indiana, on horseback. The route was planked (Territorial Road) as far as Morenci, Michigan, and was forested with Indian trails beyond that. He occasionally would be accompanied by a westward traveler as he was one early spring day in 1838, as he recalled many years later.

"I was a lad then of fourteen summers and had carried the mail for more than a year over this trail, which was one almost unbroken forest. Along the route would be a settlement or a tavern here or there where a traveller could stay all night. Travellers wishing to go West would wait at Sylvania for the 'mail boy' to pilot them over this route.

"It was in March, 1838 when a traveller, whom I was piloting through the woods, and myself left the old Territorial road and set out to the westward over these Indian trails which I had travelled many times. To me it was the same old story over again, but the fellow with me seemed to dread starting into the 'thirty-mile woods.' It was a fine March day. The sun shone warm and the snow began to melt, and by two or three o'clock it was difficult for the horses to travel.

"As we were riding along a trail on the bank of the St. Joe river near the Indiana line, the man remarked that we must be near a settlement, for he had seen a dog down in the river bottom. I told him the nearest settlement was five or six miles ahead of us, and that dog he had seen was a wolf. Along about sundown he called my attention to another wolf trotting through the woods some distance from us. I knew those wolves meant trouble for us before we reached the tavern."

It began to get dark and the traveling companion, hoping for the best perhaps, asked young John Butler if the howling they were hearing might be that of dogs. John, however, knew they were being trailed by the pack of wolves, hungry after a long winter, and it would only be a matter of time before they were upon them. They stopped just long enough to cut clubs from tree branches, then pushed their tired horses down the trail as fast as they could go.

"Nearer and nearer came the sound, until we knew they were almost upon us," John Butler recalled. "I told that man with me not to try to run from them when they came upon us but to pull up to a big tree and fight them off with his club. If he could kill one the rest of the pack would stop and eat it, and that would give us a little time to go a little further. Looking back, I could see that forms on the snow of a dozen or more wolves close to us."

The pair stopped at a large tree, each backing up to opposite sides of the trunk, and the battle began, swinging their clubs at the wolves with all their might. The woods filled with the sounds of snarling, barking wolves and the screams of the terrified horses. "For a half hour we fought those vicious beasts. Finally they retreated and we knew one of them had fallen a victim to our clubs, and that it was our chance to push on. It was only a short time before we could hear those wolves coming on again, and I knew that this fight would be harder than the other, for the taste of blood had added to the fury of those wild beasts."

Though still over two miles from the tavern that was their destination, the two took up positions again at a large oak tree. The battle began anew and, "how long we fought them off I do not know. We shouted for help and in the fierce fight our horses became frightened and attempted to break away which we knew meant certain death. When we were exhausted and almost overpowered, I heard the report of a gun and knew the tavern keeper had heard our shouts. Finally, after what seemed like hours of waiting and fighting we could see the light of a torch. It was our tavern keeper."

A few well-directed shots from the keeper's gun and the light from his torch sent the wolves into retreat and "we, half-dead, proceeded to the tavern where the good landlady did everything she could to cheer us up and make us comfortable."

John Butler and his companion were fortunate. For the tavern keeper and his wife had come to expect John on his trips and, when he didn't show, listened in the night for some sort of sound and heard the pleas for help amidst the howling of the wolves. Their concern for their young guest probably saved his life as well as that of his traveling companion.

Wolves were not the only animal young John Butler had a close encounter with. One October day in the 1830s he accompanied an early settler named Briggs on a quest to find a "bee tree" from which to gather honey along Bean Creek in what is now western Fulton County. The technique they used was to set fire to a piece of honeycomb they brought along which would attract honeybees. They would then follow the "bee line" back to the hive. They also had a second piece of honeycomb for the bees to feed on.

They selected a spot, a fire was set, the bees arrived, and Mr. Briggs followed them off through the woods, leaving John Butler to keep the comb burning, as he later recalled. "As I sat there watching the bees feed on the old comb, until they had all they could carry away, then rise a few feet in the air and start off in the direction in which I had seen Mr. Briggs leave, I heard a noise a short distance back of me. I was not startled at the sound as it was not uncommon in those days to have an Indian walk up to you without you seeing or hearing him until he spoke to you and so, being busy then fixing the fire and burning a little more comb, I did not look around."

John then heard a sniffing sound but assumed it was a deer. The sound came closer and "I thought it was time that I found out what it was making the noise. I raised up and looked around and there within ten feet of me sat a big black bear. I uttered a scream and with a bound I was going through those woods as fast as my legs would carry me."

He sprinted through the woods, and "at every bound I expected to feel the fangs of that bear sink into my flesh. I did not stop to turn around but kept on running until I reached Mr. Briggs who had heard my cries for help and had hurried back to me. Reaching me he exclaimed, 'What's the matter John?' All I could say was 'A bear.'"

John was too terrified to turn around until, finally, Mr. Briggs convinced that there was no bear in pursuit. John reluctantly accompanied him back to the spot where the honeycombs were and the one the bees had been feeding on was gone, taken by the bear. Although a bee tree had been located, they decided to call it a day and John jumped at every sound on the way back home. That night, "after I was in bed, I could see that big black bear sitting up on his hind legs looking at me. It was hours before I could go to sleep." A few days later they went back to the tree, harvested their crop, "and the honey we got out of it was enjoyed upon our corn bread for many a day."

CHAPTER IX

Coming to America

Much has been written over the years of the first generation settlers to northwest Ohio and their struggles in carving out a living from a hostile land. Some came from families that had spent a generation or two in the eastern U.S. before coming to Ohio while others came directly from Europe. For those who came directly here, that struggle frequently began as soon as they boarded a ship in Europe, especially if they were of modest means and could only afford the lower priced accommodations.

Journey From Germany

Henry Joseph Boehmer came to Ohio from Germany in late 1833, settling the following summer in Putnam County. Stopping in Cincinnati on the way, he wrote a lengthy letter to his family back home describing his voyage, his message serving as a warning as much as a greeting.

He and his wife Agnes and several family friends sailed from Bremen, Germany, on an emigrant ship Oct. 11, 1833. The first order of business was for the passengers to surrender virtually all their personal luggage, to be piled in a heap in the bowels of the ship. They then were divided into groups of 11 and assigned to a single bunk bed, six sleeping in the lower and five in the upper. The space for sleeping between the decks was about five feet high. "One can easily imagine what a miserable place the between-deck passengers had as there were 83 of us," Joseph Boehmer wrote.

"No provision whatever was made for ventilation. A small opening could have easily been made which could have been opened and closed as a means to draw out the foul air. Vinegar was supplied for fumigating a few times and at the beginning and end of the voyage. There was not a single window in the between decks and in stormy weather, when the entrance was closed, it was as dark as a walled-in subterranean prison. I believed we would all go mad if we had to sit in the dark during the long evenings and the whole night on the entire voyage." The passengers initially were not allowed to have oil lamps below decks but the ship's captain relented, after a protest, and lamps were allowed but only until 8:00 p.m.

Due to poor weather they were forced to lay over at the Isle of Wight in England. There a wind-blown ship's sail struck Agnes, breaking her collarbone. She was bandaged by a local doctor and, because of her condition, allowed to sleep in a storeroom so she could be attended to, which was a considerable improvement over the bunks. "Agnes' accident was more fortunate than a misfortune, as we were freed from between the deck, and Agnes suffered but little pain from the wound."

They sailed from the Isle of Wight Oct. 26 and over proceeding days, many of the passengers became severely seasick, many too ill to leave their bunks, the lack of ventilation only aggravating the situation. The food was poor and barely nourishing, the weather frequently stormy and, with virtually no provision for washing clothes or attending to personal hygiene, conditions merely worsened as the voyage went on. On Nov. 5, the first child of what would be several died and was sewn up in a sail cloth and thrown overboard.

Through the voyage the captain showed little concern for the welfare of his passengers and frequently spoke to them in disparaging terms. "I could fill pages if I went into details of all the odious treatment and inhumanity of our Captain Johnson, a born Swede," Boehmer wrote.

After 42 days the ship finally reached Chesapeake Bay on Dec. 7. "The sight of the land, the Paradise, was a great relief and joy to the passengers." They spent a couple of weeks in Baltimore before making their way to Cincinnati where Joseph Boehmer penned his letter. And to those back in

Germany planning to follow in his footsteps and book passage to America he warned, "Don't depend too much on the promises of the ticket agents and salesmen. Let no one be misled by the boasting, printed pamphlets."

By the summer of 1834 the Boehmers and their friends made their way to northwest Ohio and Putnam County and bought the site where Fort Jennings stood on the Auglaize River, a War of 1812 compound, and where the town of the same name was established. Joseph Boehmer went on to be a Putnam County commissioner and three-term representative in the Ohio House. He died in Fort Jennings in 1868.

Journey From England

Anna Hall, along with various family members, came from England to Ohio a couple of years prior to the Boehmers in 1832. Although they had the financial means to avoid the steerage conditions of their German compatriots, their voyage was no less fraught with trials and troubles. Anna Hall kept a diary of their trip.

August 8, 1832, she left Wallingford, a small 10th century town on the River Thames. "Left Wallingford for America with my dear mother, three brothers, four sisters and three nieces. We departed amidst the tears and, I trust, prayers of many friends and arrived on the 10th at Bristol," she wrote. Five days later, aboard the ship *Cosmo*, they sailed down the Bristol Channel and rough weather and seasickness set in almost immediately. By the 19th they were mostly too seasick to get out of bed and weather had forced them to anchor at Lundy Island, just off the British coast. There, "a poor child died during the night. The burial service was read by the captain and the corpse was committed to the mighty deep."

The ship sailed again briefly, putting in the 22nd at Milford Haven for several days on the coast of Wales where many of the passengers went ashore. Another child had died the previous night and was buried at sea discreetly so that the people of the town didn't think the ship was carrying disease, cholera in particular. They departed briefly on Sunday the 26th but the sailors ran the ship aground while singing boisterous songs at the urging of their captain. It seems they were trying to drown out the singing of religious hymns by Anna Hall and others.

The next day officials from Milford Haven told those on board they were forbidden to come to town anymore, that they believed they were all infected of cholera—a third child had died Aug. 25. On the 28th the ship finally set sail again in rough seas which brought a return of severe seasickness to the passengers. This was shadowed by the very real fear of a cholera outbreak, a dreaded disease that could kill a person in a matter of hours.

On the 29th Hall wrote, "Confined to our beds, the sailors said they never saw so much sickness on board any ship before. The stormy weather continued, a fourth child died, and on the 31st, "Very rough and wet, not able to stay on deck without clinging to ropes. Below parcels, boxes, kettles, etc. are rolling in all directions. Oh, who would wish to come to sea." The following Sunday religious services were held, but below deck. "Religion appears to be hateful to many on board. A sailor remarked that as it was Sunday, those old devils would be praying again and then we would have another storm."

On Sept. 3, a woman with cholera-like symptoms died, much to everyone's alarm. During her sea burial, a drunken, misbehaving passenger had to be lashed down by the crew. The weather broke and on the 7th, two large Portuguese warships passed by. "Spoke with one of them," Hall wrote. "They were from Bavaria, bound for Amsterdam. It seemed pleasant to speak with them so many miles from land. The sight of a stranger is a novelty."

On Sunday the 9th, in a bit of turnaround, the captain not only permitted religious services to be held on deck but encouraged the other passengers to attend, although he showed no interest personally. The rest of September contin-ued on with the weather being more favorable than not and the ship progressed on its voyage. The month being the mild one that it is, there were a number of pleasant days spent on deck.

No more passenger deaths were reported by Anna Hall after Sept. 8, four children and two adults up to that point, although there continued to be quite a bit of sickness on board. Perhaps no more death visited the ship or perhaps death became an ordinary event, one no longer noteworthy.

October dawned and the *Cosmo* neared the American shore. On the 4th it neared Sandy Hook, New Jersey, and "the sailors are dancing [and] the passengers are delighted beyond measure. The doctor has come to see that we have no disease among us. We have been told to put on our best looks, that our appearance should not oblige us to lay quarantine, and now we must march in order before his highness." The passengers passed their medical inspection before "his highness" the doctor and the ship was permitted to sail into New York harbor.

"Sailing for New York and nothing can surpass the beauty of the scenery, the number of vessels in the harbor and beautiful buildings on either side is most grateful to the eye." They docked in the city and walked ashore for the first time in their new land. That night they were too excited to sleep.

From New York City, it was up the Hudson River to Albany and the newly opened Erie Canal, regarded then as the eighth wonder of the world, and across upstate New York. Canal travel presented a somewhat different hazard, low bridges that could knock one down and in fact Hall's mother was knocked over by a bridge but not injured. As they crossed the state, their fellow canal boat passengers disembarked to begin their new lives at such places as Utica, Syracuse, Rochester, and Rome.

For the group from England it was on to Buffalo and Lake Erie. "Almost fancy we are once more on the Atlantic. Some of the passengers very sick but as we were just from off the sea, the motion of the steamer did not affect us." They disembarked at Cleveland, then down the Ohio and Erie Canal to central Ohio and Springfield where they spent a quiet Christmas, 1832, nostalgic for the Yules of home. "Christmas Day. Stayed at home and worked, there being no public worship. Indeed there is no observance of the day here whatever."

She lived for a time on a farm in Springfield and accumulated a goodly number of cattle. In 1836, now married, she and her husband walked, cattle and all, to Ottawa County and bought land near Port Clinton, and established a farm.

CHAPTER X

LIFE ON THE NORTHWEST OHIO FRONTIER

The barrier that was the Great Black Swamp delayed settlement in northwest Ohio for decades both in the actual swamp and in lands adjacent. As the majority of the more accessible and desirable lands in the region had been taken by about 1830, it wasn't until then that settlers began coming here in any numbers, willing to trade back-breaking labor and deprivation for land to farm. Two groups that came to northwest Ohio in 1834 fit into that category, one group that was the very first settlers in German Township in Fulton County, and the other among the very first settlers in Rice Township in Sandusky County.

German Township

On a hot morning in late July 1834, 43 men, women, and children with five ox teams and covered wagons left Wayne County, Ohio, for the northwest part of the state to complete the last 160 of their 4,000 mile journey from the Old World to the new. Five families were included in this group; those of Christian Lauber, Reverend Jacob Binder, John Meister, Jacob Kibbler, and John Van Gundy, a widower with four children.

They had been in Wayne County for about six weeks after arriving from both the Alsace-Lorraine region of France and from Switzerland. The Swiss and French families had lived about 50 miles apart in their native lands but had not become acquainted until they met in Wayne County. On the voyage over, the ship carrying the Swiss had actually passed that of their Alsace-Lorraine counterparts. They stayed with friends while several of the men went scouting for land, walking first to Fort Wayne, then down the Maumee River to Defiance. There they were told of an old hunter and trapper named Joseph Bates who lived about 18 miles north and knew the land. Mr. Bates led them into the heavily forested and marshy wilds of what would become Fulton County to a point where the land rose a bit and they liked what they saw. They liked what they saw not because they relished the brutal labor of turning wilderness into farmland but because they were nonconformists, Amish-Mennonites, and they wanted a place where they could grow their own physical as well as spiritual community. From there they walked to the U.S. land office in Wapakoneta, staked a claim for 800 acres, then headed back to Wayne County.

The heat of July became the dog days of August, the lurching of the wagons and clouds of dust their constant companions. They came to Perrysburg and crossed the bridgeless Maumee River, the Reverend Binder almost losing his wagon in the process. They traveled the river trail and stopped for the night in the now ghost town of Providence across from present-day Grand Rapids. There John Van Gundy gathered wood for fire while a young son called to him. Suddenly the child lay dead, neither the grief-stricken father or any other members of the party having observed any previous symptoms. They continued on to Napoleon, arriving there 16 days after leaving Wayne County, where they were quite disappointed to find only one cabin in a city with such a famous name. The land that they had staked claim to lay 22 miles to the north and west but the only trail that would take them there would be the one they would hack themselves.

With a government surveyor recruited from Defiance to guide them, a group of eight went ahead to blaze a trail through the woods. They missed their mark and sent two of the men back to Napoleon for more food while the remaining six and the surveyor continued on. They finally reached their spot at dark of the second day and, with no food or shelter, huddled around a fire while a fierce thunderstorm lashed the dark and towering, virgin woods much of the night. They headed back to Napoleon the next day, gratefully meeting the other two, who were returning with food, to find six of the party sick with the dreaded Black Swamp fever or ague, with its accompanying fever, chills, and uncontrollable shaking. They left anyway and with all able-bodied members of the group clearing a primitive road, they made two miles a day, the sick ones laying in the wagons. Eleven mosquito-plagued days later they reached their land; untouched wilderness with the nearest settlement, Maumee, a three-day journey away. They were strangers in a strange land, unfamiliar with its language or customs, and with no previous experience in the rigors of life in the wilderness. The date was Aug. 22, and if they were going to have a roof over their heads for the winter they had better get busy.

Having only their wagons and huts made of brush and leaves for shelter, they felled trees in earnest and all managed to get a cabin or shelter built. Christian Lauber built a large 20 by 24 foot cabin on the high point of the land, which came to be known as Lauber Hill, while the others built in a ring around it. The Reverend Binder, due to constant illness, was only able to get something up about half that size with a partially dirt floor and no chimney to properly vent smoke from the fireplace. By spring he and his family had taken on the color of smoked ham.

It would be a long winter for all with no crop in the ground or farm animals. Before year's end, two of John Meister's sons, aged 21 and 12, died of disease. Food was scarce and boiled bran and water became part of the daily diet along with wild weeds and nuts. The men brought no hunting skills or firearms with them, so the only meat they had was the occasional starved and frozen rabbit or raccoon.

But somehow they persevered and the following year they planted crops between the stumps of felled trees. Digging out the stumps of these great trees was beyond question until they had been allowed to rot for a few years. Grass and hay for the oxen and their few acquired cattle were scarce and trees were felled so they could feed on the leaves.

The nearest mill and market was in Maumee by way of Napoleon, about a 45-mile journey over terrible roads, if they could be called that. On the return from one of these journeys the exhausted oxen reached a nearby creek, crossed part of the way, and refused to go further, Christian Lauber and another settler giving up and leaving them there. When they returned the next day their tails had frozen fast in the ice which they had to break up before driving the oxen home.

Through the 1830s more stout-hearted men, women, and families came and in 1839 the Lucas County commissioners established German Township—Fulton County would not exist until 1850. The rise in the land that is still known as Lauber Hill today can be seen at the intersection of County Road 21 and U.S. 20-A in Fulton County. On the county road stands Lauber Hill Reformed Mennonite Church, circa 1865, and a cemetery where Christian Lauber and others who made the arduous journey here in 1834 now rest in peace.

Rice Township

It was the 28th day of June, 1834, and five families bade farewell to their village of Voerstetten in Germany, leaving the motherland behind forever. Early September found them in New York City where they were less than impressed. "Hogs, cattle and horses were running at large in the streets. The whole city seemed to be a pasture lot," recalled George Engler, Jr., one of the group who was 12 years-old at the time. From there they took a water route to Ohio; the Hudson River to the Erie Canal to Lake Erie, arriving by steamer in Sandusky, then called Portland.

"On our arrival there we found the town deserted, as the cholera was raging there. Most of the people had left town." From Sandusky they walked to Lower Sandusky (Fremont) and found it also virtually deserted for the same reason. (The 1834 cholera epidemic that swept through the area began in Marblehead, when residents there dragged ashore victims of the disease that had been tossed off a passing ship in order to give them a proper burial.) None of the few remaining residents of the town spoke German so the group built a fire under an oak tree and spent the night on the ground. In the morning a "colored man" named Vincent Curtice found them, and took them to his home where he and his wife provided breakfast.

The brother of George Engler's father, Martin Engler, had preceded them by a year. They found him the next day and now had a place to stay. After being there a couple of days they were called out at midnight to bury the body of a neighbor who had died of cholera. "Uncle Martin and father buried him on his farm, in the woods, by torchlight. They had no fears of burying a man who died of cholera than of any other disease and thought nothing of it." Uncle Martin split his 80 acres with his brother who, by November, had built a cabin complete with basswood furniture; "not very handsome but strong and durable."

They spent the winter clearing land, Black Swamp turf that had been high and dry in the fall but was knee deep in water in the spring. So father and son scraped the soil into mounds, planted seed corn, and waited. After about a week "we examined the hills and found the corn all gone. The squirrels had dug it up and carried it away." It was a rough start to what would be a rough few years.

When corn was finally grown it was milled at home my means of a "pouncer," a heavy, wooden hammer suspended from a spring pole. The corn would be placed on top of a solid, oak stump that had been chiseled out to the shape of a bowl and pounded. What could be sifted through was used to make bread while the rest was fed to livestock.

In addition to cornbread, the settlers diet in the early years consisted heavily of wild game. Venison, wild turkey, pheasant, quail, squirrel, rabbit, and fish from the Sandusky River were regular, if not tiresome, items of fare on early Rice Township dinner tables. A barrel of salted white bass, catfish, or pickerel could be had for two dollars. Fifty cents could get you two hind quarters of venison. A large wild turkey or a dozen pheasants went for a quarter while quails were priced at a penny.

By the fall and winter of 1836, things were getting desperate for the Englers and their German neighbors in Rice Township, about 14 families in all. "The money they had brought from Germany was all spent in paying for their land, houses and living or subsistence for two years; they had but little land cleared, the crops were poor, everything was high that they had to buy. . . . You could not go to a neighbor's and borrow a bushel of wheat or corn as they were about all in the same situation."

About that time along came a savior of sorts, a man named Jacob Bowlus who had come to the county in 1822, which was quite early, and was well established. He had heard of the struggling German colony and came to see what he could do to help. He had a large farm and sawmill operation on Muskellunge Creek and gave many of them work, paying mostly in food and other provisions. He also was a United Brethren preacher who was fluent in German.

Even though the settlers were Catholics and Lutherans, they readily joined his congregation. "Our German settlers hadn't heard a German sermon for several years, it was something new to them and reminded them of old times long gone by. . . . Mr. Bowlus' sermons gave the people new hope and energy which did much good in the settlement. . . . He practiced what he preached and I don't know what in the world some of our people would have done if it hadn't been for him. All honor to that grand old man."

An artistic rendering by Norma Thomas-Herr shows what the first cabin built on Lauber Hill by Christian Lauber in 1834 looked like. The area is now German Township in Fulton County. (Courtesy of Sauder Village, Archbold, Ohio.)

In Lauber Hill Cemetery, the grave of Christian Lauber who was part of a group of pioneers who built homes in the wilderness in present-day Fulton County in 1834.

CHAPTER XI

Wood County Wanderer

In western Wood County in the one-time heart of the Great Black Swamp, a stone marker rises from Weston Cemetery on the edge of the village of Weston. Its epitaph, now faded by time, memorializes one who was born but does not rest there.

> *Our Brother*
> *Ralph Keeler*
> *Born August 28, 1840;*
> *Supposed to have been lost*
> *at sea*
> *December 14, 1873*

The few and mysterious words of the stone, which must have intrigued many who read it over the years, provide scant clue to what was a remarkable but little-known Wood County native, one who might have achieved literary prominence had his life not ended prematurely on a dark, December night on a steamship off the Cuban coast.

The details of Ralph Keeler's early days are sketchy but what is known is that he was born in 1840, the youngest of five children on a Wood County grassland, known as Keeler's Prairie, named for his father who raised cattle there. However his father died the day after Ralph's fourth birthday and his mother a few years after that, which broke up the family.

The older children went to live elsewhere while young Ralph remained home under the care of a guardian, where he was not happy.

The intelligent and restless Ralph left his home at the age of eight and walked to Toledo where he had relatives; his grandfather was a War of 1812 veteran and early Toledo settler. At the age of nine he was sent way to school in Buffalo. At age 11 he slipped away from the school, found work on a Lake Erie steamer, and was taken in by the ship's steward and his wife, a childless couple, who lived in Conneaut. Despite being showered with affection by the steward's wife, he left after two weeks. He returned to Toledo, taking care to avoid relatives who might be searching for him.

The next chapter in his life was spent hiring out as a cabin boy to various ships sailing out of Toledo, always staying independent and never seeking shelter with family. At one point he returned to Buffalo briefly where he had been exposed to, and fascinated by, minstrel shows. He decided then he would become a minstrel performer. He worked hard on his craft; singing, dancing (he nailed pennies to the heels of his shoes for taps), and playing instruments and frequently being chased from Toledo rooming houses for the racket he was making. He finally caught the notice of a local minstrel manager who put him on stage and within a week his performances were popular and being advertised on a banner strung across Summit Street in downtown Toledo.

His success brought him to Cincinnati where he was hired to perform on Mississippi riverboats, which he did for three years, usually performing in blackface. He later wrote of his experiences for the *Atlantic Monthly* magazine, in "My Three Years as a Negro Minstrel." He attended St. Vincent's College in Missouri for over a year, a school that he observed from a passing riverboat and talked his way into. He then attended Kenyon College in Gambier, Ohio, earning money while there by writing articles for the *Toledo Daily Blade*, as it was then known, as well as other Toledo newspapers. He left Kenyon at the end of his junior year, returned to Toledo, and worked briefly in the post office. He accumulated savings of $181, and decided to tour Europe on that amount. He did so by traveling on foot in the garb of an itinerant worker, meeting people and making friends—he spoke seven languages—and staying at country inns for as little as four cents per night. He wrote of his experiences for the *Atlantic* as well, in "A Tour of Europe for $181 in Currency."

His next venture found him in California writing a novel and working as a journalist and a lecturer. There he became friends with a man named Samuel Clemens, better known as Mark Twain. Both shared a love for writing and for the Mississippi River. Later, when both were in Boston, Ralph would travel with Twain on the lecture circuit and at one point hosted a luncheon for him and other luminaries of the Boston literary scene, who, like Twain, had sort of adopted him. A Mark Twain biographer described Keeler as "an eccentric, gifted and altogether charming fellow . . . poor of purse but inexhaustibly rich in the happier gifts of fortune. He was unfailingly buoyant, light-hearted and hopeful."

The novel Ralph Keeler had written in California was not very well received. However the biographer relates a story of Keeler rushing to Twain's Boston hotel room one day and having him hurry with him to the local library. There, a beaming Ralph pointed out that not only was his novel on the shelf but, according to library records, it had been checked out three times in two years! "Knowing Mark Twain," the biographer wrote, "his eyes were likely to be filled with tears."

While traveling the lecture circuit on his own, Keeler regularly visited family in Toledo and in Weston and Custar in Wood County. In 1869, he achieved a boyhood dream when he became a staffer on the *Atlantic*. In 1873, the last year of his life, he was in Toledo in the summer for the wedding of an aunt and spent some time at Kelley's Island in Lake Erie. He was then working as a correspondent for the *New York Tribune*. At the time a revolt was taking place in Cuba against the ruling Spanish government when a ship with an American and British crew, and flying the American flag, was seized in late October off the Cuban coast by Spanish authorities. The ship was carrying arms and rebel sympathizers to the island. The seizure of the vessel, and the resulting trials and executions of some of the ship's crew and passengers, created a period of brief but high tension between the United States and Spain.

Ralph Keeler was sent by the *Tribune* on Nov. 25 to Cuba to investigate the matter, a major and potentially dangerous assignment. While in Santiago de Cuba, where the trials and executions were taking place, he became apprehensive that he was being followed by Spanish agents and was allowed to board the U.S. Navy ship, *Juniata*, which was docked there, for his own protection. He remained aboard for several days.

On Dec. 14, probably restless and itching to get a story, he left the navy ship and boarded a mail steamer for Havana. He was never seen again. The mail ship's crew discovered him missing the morning of the 15th and assumed he fell overboard; the ship's captain claimed he had seen him about midnight the night before having a glass of cognac. The commander of the *Juniata* believed he was murdered and thrown overboard by Spanish agents who were trailing him, given everything that was going on at the time, an opinion shared by Keeler's friends, family, and coworkers. Word reached back to Toledo as an article in the Dec. 29 issue of the *Toledo Daily Blade* noted, "Great apprehension is felt that Ralph Keeler, who it will be remembered went from here in November as a special correspondent of the New York *Tribune*, has been drowned in the Caribbean Sea."

The State Department investigated but, with no body found and no witnesses to his disappearance, there was little that could be determined. It seems unlikely, but not impossible, that Ralph Keeler, an experienced sea traveler on the Great Lakes, the Mississippi River, and twice over the Atlantic Ocean to Europe, would fall overboard. The sad irony, if he was murdered, is that at the time of his death, the U.S. and Spanish governments were wrapping up a diplomatic solution to the situation. In fact, within four days of Keeler's death, both the rebel ship and its remaining passengers and crew were released back to the United States, thus ending the crisis.

Thus the short but eventful story of Ralph Keeler came to an end. Grieving family members, with no closure, carved his name on the family monument in Weston Cemetery, on land once known as Keeler's Prairie near where his life began, along with the message of his mysterious end. Time and the elements have since almost completely erased the monument's inscriptions.

He left behind an autobiography of sorts, published in 1870, of the first 22 years of his life titled *Vagabond Adventures*. To those restless youngsters thinking of following in his footsteps, he starts with this bit of advice, "It may be laid down as a general principle, to start with, that a boy better not run away from home."

CHAPTER XII

NINETEENTH CENTURY CRIMES

Crimes and criminal activity may seem to be more a product of modern times but history records no lack of such behavior.

Williams County Outrage

Perhaps no crime is as heinous as that of the murder of a child, and such a crime took place in Williams County in 1847. There was an itinerant fortune teller named Andrew Tyler who drifted into the county in late spring of that year and drifted from farm to farm, telling fortunes with cards. He stopped at the farm of Peter Schamp, a farmer and shoemaker who lived near the present-day village of West Unity. He concluded that Peter Schamp had money and came up with the idea of kidnapping and murdering his four-year-old son David, hiding the body, then getting paid a sum of money to use his alleged fortune-telling talent to lead searchers to the remains.

In order to lure young David away from the farm Tyler recruited a local teenager named Daniel Heckerthorne, described as "half-witted" and an "imbecile," promising him a share of the money if he helped out. On Sunday, June 13, Heckerthorne did as he was instructed and David was taken to the woods and fed candy laced with strychnine. When the child became upset and began to cry, Heckerthorne grabbed him by the heels and dashed his head against a beech tree, killing him. One account says Tyler was present, another says he was not, that Heckerthorne killed the boy alone as instructed by Tyler and hid the body near a stream inside a hollow log.

When it was discovered that David was missing, search teams were organized with Tyler leading one of the teams himself, claiming his fortune-telling skills gave him the advantage, and that he had "visions" of the child's body being near water and covered with rotting wood. They hunted Sunday and Monday with no luck and the searchers working with Tyler noticed he kept directing them away from a certain area and began to suspect something was up. On Tuesday the search team told Tyler they suspected him, and returned to the area without him and found the body. Meanwhile both Tyler and Heckerthorne were trying to flee the county, but were soon caught. Several of those apprehending Tyler wanted to hang him on the spot but cooler heads prevailed. Heckerthorne may have confessed immediately, accounts disagree on this, although they agree that Tyler adamantly, and even arrogantly, maintained his innocence

They were taken to the old, log jail in Bryan, which was then little more than a frontier settlement, but were transferred to a larger and more secure jail in Maumee for their own protection. Tyler demanded a trial before the Ohio Supreme Court, which then traveled a circuit to each county. The trial would not take place until July of the following year when the court made its scheduled stop in Williams County.

They returned to Bryan as scheduled and Tyler was tried first, found guilty on July 25, 1848, and sentenced to death. Heckerthorne was tried later and given the same sentence which was commuted to life in prison by the governor as he was "so plainly an imbecile." Tyler's execution was set for the following January and it is written that he refused to believe that he would actually be executed, that it was all some sort of hoax, even laughing and joking with carpenters who came to build the gallows outside the Bryan log jail. The Williams County sheriff had a tall privacy fence built around the gallows, in compliance with state law, but the night before the execution a crowd determined to witness the event tore the fence down, burning the wood to keep warm.

They also were determined that Tyler would get no rest on his final night on Earth and, with many in the crowd drinking, cursed and yelled all night long.

On the day of the hanging, an estimated 3,000 people came to Bryan to see it, nearly half the county's population at the time, a number that might have been larger had travel not been made difficult by a January thaw which sent area streams out of their banks. The sheriff had previously sent for companies of State Guards to keep order, anticipating that such a large crowd would show.

On Friday the 26th, Friday being the traditional Hangman's Day, the guards marched into town to the sound of fife and drums and Andrew Tyler was led to the gallows. A shroud was placed over his head and a noose around his neck, the gallows trap was sprung, and his body dropped through. However he had worked the rope up around his chin and left ear, and he swung about kicking and struggling. The rope was adjusted and he was dropped through a second time which brought about his end. He died without expressing any regret or remorse.

Afterwards his remains were dissected and kept in a barrel in the hall of the jail, the container having a loose lid so the curious could look in. They were moved a couple of times after that, even ending up briefly in the hands of some mischievous schoolboys. There's no record that the remains of Andrew Tyler were ever actually buried. The written accounts give no reason why Tyler's remains were treated as they were. One can only assume it was a show of complete contempt for someone who would murder a child in order to extort a few dollars from his father.

Daniel Heckerthorne was paroled in 1860 from the Ohio State Penitentiary, never to return to Williams County although one account states he died of old age in the pen. Perhaps he was paroled and later returned.

Young David Schamp was buried on the farm and later reinterred in a family plot in Floral Grove Cemetery near West Unity. There he rests in a quiet, country cemetery near an old church, his gravestone giving no clue of a how an innocent young life came to such an awful end.

A Thief Extraordinaire

Also from the county of Williams comes the tale of a widow with two small children who was soon to be evicted from her land for inability to pay the mortgage. This was weighing heavily on her mind when a mysterious stranger knocked on her cabin door on a late afternoon in autumn, 1840. He asked for a meal and a place to stay for the night which she refused. However he was both persistent and charming so she took him in.

During supper she mentioned her woes and that her debt was $500 and that soon she and her children would have nowhere to go. The stranger listened quietly then retired for the evening, insisting he sleep on a couch near the door. The next morning she arose to make him breakfast but he and his horse were gone. On the table was a note thanking her for her hospitality and some money; exactly $500.

Shortly thereafter the sheriff and a posse came thundering up, wanting to know if she had seen a man who fit the description of her guest. When she described the man who had stayed there the sheriff yelled, "Do you know who you kept in your house?" When the woman replied that she did not, he said "Well that was Sile Doty, the notorious horse thief!"

While the above tale may be a bit embellished, Silas "Sile" Doty was anything but. He lived to steal and stole to live. A retrospective article in the *Toledo News-Bee* newspaper in 1937 described him as "Toledo's original Public Enemy No. 1 . . . [a] robber baron extraordinary, the bane—sometimes the blessing, depending on the point of view—of the whole northwestern Ohio frontier." However the 19th century thief did not merely limit his practice to northwest Ohio. His sticky-fingered ways took him to New England, the Midwest, the West, Canada, Mexico and even England. One of the secrets to his success was that there were few jails that could hold him. In fact the reason the Williams County posse was chasing him was because he had escaped from the jail in the county seat of Bryan after being arrested trying to sell a stolen horse.

When Sile Doty was an old man he gave a series of interviews detailing his life of crime before dying in 1876; a book on his life was published in Toledo in 1880. It was said that in later years it was difficult to find a copy of the book as his embarrassed descendants bought up as many copies as they could find and burned them.

He was born in Vermont in 1800 to religious parents, his mother giving him many lectures on the importance of being good and honest, instruction that went unheard. As a small child he enjoyed stealing playthings from his brothers and sisters and hiding them where they could not be found. He spent his youth and early adulthood plying his craft in New England, parts of eastern Canada, and England.

He was adept at staying one step ahead of the law and became skilled at the blacksmithing and metal working arts, producing quality files and saws that could cut through any kind of iron. These he used for breaking into buildings, and for sawing his way out of jail on the occasions he was caught. He also made keys that would fit most locks and produced quality sets of handcuffs he would sell to local sheriffs, keeping extra sets of keys for himself and his crooked friends. And wherever he went he was adept at identifying others who, like him, had criminal tendencies.

In spring 1834, needing some fresh territory to work, he relocated to Adrian, Michigan, and was pleased to find, "this region infested with rascals of very grade." He soon became leader of a loose gang of outlaws that stretched from Chicago to Cleveland. He relocated to Detroit for a time and made good money smuggling liquor and other goods from Canada, roaming as far east as Buffalo and west to Chicago on various kinds of stealing expeditions.

In 1837 he returned to the Adrian area, in part because his wife was unhappy at his long absences and the extensive night hours his occupation required. Back in Adrian, he rented land and tried to live the life of an honest farmer. But by summer with the forests thick with growth and the grass growing high, conditions perfect for hiding and feeding stolen horses, he returned to his old ways. He went back to Detroit after a pair of fine, black horses he had seen while there, stole the steeds, and made his way back toward Adrian, where he was caught by a group of five pursuers. He fled on foot into the woods, saving himself but losing his prize horses. Most crooks might have been satisfied with escaping arrest but not Sile Doty.

He followed the men back to Adrian, where they stopped at a tavern to drink and brag about their exploits, then stole the horses again. "I knew then just where I was and where to go." And that was for the wilds of the Great Black Swamp which then was just beginning to be settled. He crossed the Maumee River at Perrysburg, hiring someone to take one of the horses in advance so as to not arouse the suspicion of the bridge gatekeeper. He then went about six miles beyond, well into the Swamp, to the home of a cohort where he hid out about a week; "one of the safest places I was ever in, as it was surrounded by the thickest wood I ever saw, for miles around." He eventually ended up in Columbus where he sold the horses for $250, a nice piece of change in those days.

He walked to Delaware, Ohio, to the home of another crime partner, who helped him steal another horse, then headed back to Perrysburg, paying a boy 50 cents to take his horse to a hotel in Maumee, less the toll collector see him so soon on a different mount. He made it back to Michigan, but having been gone 20 days, faced an angry wife, who was rapidly becoming disenchanted with him. He tried resuming the farm life, but it wouldn't last.

He hit the road in fall, 1838, on a horse-stealing trip, ending up in Kentucky where he stole a pair of race horses. He dozed off while hiding in some woods and was startled when approached by a black man, a local slave named Pompey. Doty told him he would help him escape to Ohio, if he was willing to take the risk. The slave went back to the plantation for clothes, a saddle, and to bid his wife goodbye. They made it to Ohio where, "As soon as we landed, I saw a marked change come over Pomp's face. I thought it must be the inhaling of free air; he looked larger and more of a man than he did on the Kentucky side." They rode into Indiana where Pompey was left at the home of an abolitionist in Richmond.

In 1839, he moved his family to Indiana and in the next few years things would slowly unravel. He hired a farmhand there and the two did not get along. After an argument, the farmhand left saying he was going to tell authorities of Doty's crimes and Sile followed him to talk him out of it. Things got heated and Doty struck him with his cane and killing him, unintentionally he claimed. He hid the body but when it was found a couple of years later he was charged and convicted in Fort Wayne of second degree murder in 1844 and sentenced to life in state prison at hard labor.

In 1846 he won an appeal for a second trial and was brought to the county jail in Angola, Indiana, where he escaped, was caught, and escaped again, this time heading to Mexico to join the U.S. Army in the Mexican War. Perhaps Doty's time in prison had embittered him—on the way to Mexico he lingered near the state prison in Indiana for the opportunity, which never came, to murder the warden who he claimed abused him.

While in Mexico he caught on with the army as a cook and later as a waiter for General Winfield Scott after he presented him with a fine, and of course stolen, horse (Scott is the stuff of army legend having served as a general nearly 50 years from the War of 1812 to the early days of the Civil War.) In Mexico Doty was not the charming and sometimes generous thief of local lore but a strong-armed mugger and even murderer, working with a gang of thugs who took advantage of the chaos of wartime conditions. He told of these misdeeds to his late-life interviewer without expressing any contrition.

The war ended in 1848 and he returned to Michigan, relocating near Coldwater, working sometimes as a shoemaker but mostly as a thief. As in the past he kept his illegal activities secret from his immediate neighbors and frequently shared his spoils with them, especially the ones in need. In 1851 he was tried and convicted in Hillsdale County on the charge of petty larceny, and his past caught up with him as the fed-up judge sentenced him to 17 years in the state prison in Jackson. He was released a couple years early in 1866, gray-haired and aging, but not too old to steal. He would be sent back to Jackson two more times spending a total of 20 of his last 25 years of his life locked up.

He stole right up to then end, giving his last interview to early March 1876 and dying on the 12th of that month. Curiously, his obituary in the *Angola Herald* read: "Death of a Wonderful Man. Silas Doty departed this life on last Sunday at the residence of his son at Reading, Michigan at the advanced age of seventy-six years. Wonderful Man! What an eventful life!"

An obituary in the *Hillsdale Standard* was more circumspect noting that he was a thief who had spent many years in prison but, "he was not without the noble traits of character and he is reported to have many times relived the wants of the suffering, even if in doing he was so obliged to commit an act upon another which jeopardized his personal liberty. Death covers a multitude of sins. Let the mantle of charity be thrown around his memory. Peace to his ashes."

Grave of four-year-old David Schamp in Floral Grove Cemetery near West Unity. The boy met a terrible end at the hands of an itinerant fortune-teller in Williams County in 1847.

CHAPTER XIII

NAPOLEON'S WOE: DEATH ON CHRISTMAS EVE

There is perhaps no more festive evening during the course of the year in this and many other countries than Christmas Eve and such was the case in Napoleon, the seat of Henry County, in 1880. However in a darkened, downtown drugstore near midnight the mood was anything but merry as an argument between and older and a younger man grew more and more heated. Voices became louder and louder, a shot rang out, and the younger man fell to the floor, blood flowing from a fatal gunshot wound to the head. What would shock not only the community of Napoleon but catch the attention of the nation was that the smoking gun was held not by a local ruffian but by a respected local businessman whose resume included such esteemed positions as physician, Civil War major general, and two-term governor of South Carolina, Robert Kingston Scott.

Robert Scott was born in Pennsylvania in 1826, his father having served in the War of 1812 and his grandfather in the American Revolution. He came to Ohio to live with a sister in 1841. Scott attended medical school in Columbus, and as a young man roamed to such places as California, Mexico, and South America. He eventually settled in the Henry County hamlet of Florida on the Maumee River where he practiced medicine for five years then moved to Napoleon in 1860 to pursue business interests.

When the Civil War broke out the following year, he threw himself full-time into recruiting soldiers and organized and eventually commanded the 68th Ohio Volunteer Infantry, a primarily Henry County regiment. He eventually rose to the rank of colonel and was given command of a brigade. On July 22, 1864 he was captured during the Atlanta campaign in the same action where General James McPherson of Clyde, Ohio, was killed, the highest ranking Union officer to die in the war. He escaped by jumping from a moving railroad boxcar, and rolling down an embankment, incurring a painful back injury in the process. After more than a week trying to make it back to Union lines, he was captured again and paroled in September. He resumed command of his brigade and took part in Sherman's historic "March to the Sea" which wrapped up in late December.

By the time the war ended the following April, Scott had been promoted to brigadier general, and after the war, to brevet major general, an honorary rank typically bestowed for service and good conduct. He returned to Napoleon briefly before being assigned commissioner of the Freedmen's Bureau in Charleston, South Carolina. He served in that position for two and a half years, and was credited for the building of schools to educate the children of former slaves. In 1868, he was elected governor of the state and was reelected to a second, two-year term in 1870. His gubernatorial terms in chaotic, postwar South Carolina were tumultuous and characterized by allegations of corruption and an attempted impeachment. Although retired from the military when first elected, he still represented to many, if not most South Carolinians, a conquering and occupying army in what was one of the most rabid states of the Confederacy. The dividing line between truth and cutthroat politics would be impossible to determine.

Robert Scott eventually came back to Napoleon, in 1878 with his wife and teenaged son, where the family had real estate interests. At six feet, two inches in height, an erect bearing, and a noteworthy list of accomplishments, the former general and governor was an impressive figure about town.

But as Christmas Eve 1880 drew nigh, not all was well in the Scott household. His wife, Rebecca, was an invalid, his

15-year-old son Robert Scott, Jr. (known as "Arkie" according historical accounts but "Archie" in the newspapers of the day), was home from school and carousing about town playing billiards and drinking. Scott himself was trying to withdraw from longtime opium use which he began after he injured his spine during his Civil War escape. Late Christmas Eve found Archie absent from the downtown hotel the family was using as a residence, hanging out and drinking with a 23-year-old man named Warren Drury. Both parents were upset by this and Robert Scott went out just before midnight to find his son after being told he was in Drury's apartment above Kneeland's Drug Store where Drury was employed.

Exactly what happened next is a bit murky but there was a confrontation between Scott and Drury at the drug store when the latter insisted that Archie was not there. Scott gained entrance to the store but was told he could not go upstairs and check for himself. Both parties became increasingly agitated and Drury allegedly told Scott that if he tried to force his way up, he would do so at his own risk and allegedly made a motion toward his back and hip. It was then that Robert Scott pulled a pistol from his overcoat pocket and shot Warren Drury at close range just under his left ear.

Scott pushed passed the body went upstairs and recovered his intoxicated son who had gone to bed, then returned to the hotel telling others what had happened and urging they go aid the mortally wounded Warren Drury. He then turned his gun over to the hotel proprietor and awaited the arrival of the sheriff. The next morning the shocking news raced through Napoleon, according to the local weekly newspaper, *The Democratic Northwest* in an article that carried the headline, "Napoleon's Woe: The Scott-Drury Tragedy!"

"Our citizens awoke from their slumber last Saturday to behold a beautiful Christmas morning looking forward to a pleasant and merry time during day. But what was their horror and dismay upon leaving their peaceful homes to learn that a terrible tragedy had taken place in their midst between the hours of twelve and one o'clock during the night," the newspaper lamented. "Had a thunder bolt exploded at their feet they would have not been more startled and shocked or their faces wore a more horrified expression; the beautiful merry Christmas morning seemed no longer beautiful and merry to them, but was transformed into a morning of sadness and gloom."

That Christmas day, Napoleon was awash with rumors and speculation. People seeking information gathered in groups that at times swelled to hundreds and there was a good deal of anger in the air. Warren Drury was a well-regarded young man who was to have been married a few days after Christmas to the daughter of the Pittsburgh, Penn., superintendent of schools. The news spread about the country as well when *The New York Times* ran an article on the incident Dec. 26. The article was more than 1,000 words in length, on page one under the headline, "Caused By A Drunken Son," and detailed both the shooting and Scott's military and political career.

Robert Scott was arrested and charged with murder in the first degree and was sent to the Defiance County jail, because the Henry County Courthouse and jail had recently burned. After a coroner's inquest, Warren Drury's body was taken back to his native Elmore, Ohio, and buried. The results of the coroner's inquest were printed in a long column adjacent to the crime story in *The Democratic Northwest* and in the column adjacent to that, coincidentally or not, was an ad reminding readers that "the finest line of toilet sets, box perfumes, brushes, paper, cut glass goods, lamps, etc." could be found at Kneeland's Drug Store.

Things settled down and Scott was not released on bail until February. His trial would not take place until the following fall during which time Napoleon was divided along pro and anti-Scott lines. The trial began Oct. 25 with Scott refusing to seek a change of venue or a continuation as his attorneys advised. A second floor meeting hall served as a temporary Henry County courtroom and was filled with a standing-room only crowd which at times stretched down the stairs. They listened as the owner of the drug store, C. A. Kneeland, testified that on the night in question, Archie had been drinking heavily and that Drury was only trying to protect him from the wrath of his father of whom he was afraid. Scott and his defense team insisted that the shooting was both accidental and unintentional;

that Scott had pulled the gun only because he thought Drury reaching for one and that, when the gun fired, Scott was so surprised he turned around and looked because he thought someone standing behind him had fired one.

Testimony from friends of Scott was admitted into evidence at the trial as well. A former political opponent in South Carolina wrote: "We ex-rebels down here, perhaps, know Scott as well as you people in Ohio do. In the hour of his distinction, and our humiliation, he came among us not to domineer over a conquered foe, but to lighten our afflictions. . . . We down here believe Scott to be innocent of the crime of murder, and none will rejoice more at his acquittal than his admirers in South Carolina." A Civil War captain from Indiana who served under him penned; "He devoted over one-half of his salary to works of charity among the widows and children of Confederate soldiers, who remember him with warm expressions of regard and some whom I learn have written in this dark hour of trial, tendering him words of confidence, sympathy and love. A brave man, a kind, loving father, a noble, trusting friend—such a man is Robert K. Scott, and such a man *cannot be a murderer*." And from a lawyer in South Carolina; "I *know* it was an accident, one of those mysterious accidents which God permits for some wise purpose."

Attorney John McSweeney led Scott's five-lawyer defense team and his summation was praised by *The Northwest Democratic*, citing his "matchless oratory" and "words of the deepest eloquence." On Friday, Nov. 4, 1881, the matter was handed over to the jury which was out all night. After asking for further instructions from the judge the following morning, the jury came back with its verdict before lunch: Not Guilty. If there was any sort of outcry in the courtroom following the verdict, the reporters covering the trial did not indicate so. In fact, a small article on the trial's outcome in *The New York Times* the following day concluded with, "The verdict appears to give general satisfaction."

However one historical account maintains that at some point after the trial a group of men from Toledo called "The Roughs" made clear their intentions to come to Napoleon and administer vigilante-style justice to Robert Scott. The Roughs boarded a train bound for Napoleon but when the train reached Maumee, an anonymous gift of two barrels of whiskey was brought aboard. And by the time the train reached Liberty Center, the men had lost their focus.

What ultimately was in Robert Scott's heart and mind that late Christmas Eve when he pulled the trigger on the gun that killed Warren Drury was known only to him. He was a man capable of kindness and compassion as testimony during the trial indicated, so one might safely assume the tragic death of a young man by his hand haunted him. The matter eventually faded from public imagination and Robert Scott would live 20 more years. He died in 1900 at the age of 74 and was buried in Glenwood Cemetery in Napoleon. He was regarded with mixed emotions in town: a street was named after him but a proposal to name a city park for him was protested and defeated.

Lost, perhaps, in the controversy and speculation that surrounds any tragic event involving a high-profile figure is the human impact. Warren Drury's grieving mother, who called her son "Warrie," addressed a letter to the citizens and young people of Napoleon: "I desire to render to you my heartfelt thanks for the kindness and many tokens of friendship shown my boy during his brief stay among you. He has spoken in the highest terms of your place and the many kind friends whom he met there. . . . I shall always remember you with feelings of the deepest friendship for the love and respect you gave my boy, and that you gave so much to make his young life happy in his associations among you. But the cold snow that covers his grave is a fit emblem of my poor heart and what my future life will be without my darling boy. Cold, bitter, bitter, cold."

Robert Kingston Scott, Civil War major general and post-war governor of South Carolina, shot a man to death on Christmas Eve in Napoleon in 1880.

Robert Scott's impressive life achievements are noted on his burial vault in Glenwood Cemetery in Napoleon.

CHAPTER XIV

BLACK SWAMP "FORREST"

Much of northwest Ohio was once covered by a vast, slumbering marsh that came to be known as the Great Black Swamp. A blend of open marshland, wild brushy growth, and majestic dark forests, it covered all or part of 12 counties in northwest Ohio including the whole of Wood and Paulding counties. It was an impediment to settlement, remaining untouched and pristine for decades while lands around it were being lumbered and drained by pioneers to create farmland and space for cities and towns.

As the country grew and the demand for land increased, the Swamp too was finally altered, its waters drained and its trees cut down—very few of its tens of thousands of acres were left in their original or near-original state. And Paulding County was no different as it developed because the land there was transformed into a green quilt of productive farmland in what became a lightly populated, agricultural county.

But there was an exception—an 80-acre stand of rolling woods that was preserved by its owners over the years. Tucked out of sight in a rural part of a rural county, its existence was known only to those who lived near it. Its most recent owner, Clair Forrest, bought it in the 1950s and it was his desire that the land lay forever in its natural state. When he died in 2003 his family sold the land to the Black Swamp Conservancy, a land trust based in Perrysburg, which used monies made available through the Clean Ohio Fund. The tract has since been named the Forrest Woods Nature Preserve.

With additional land acquisitions increasing the size of the preserve to around 250 acres, the mix of old and young woods is one of the largest such stands in northwest Ohio. Only the Oak Openings region in Lucas and Fulton counties is of similar size. While the older woods are not considered virgin, the floodplain areas in particular contain significant old-growth timber. The floodplains were carved by Marie DeLarme Creek which drains the northwestern corner of Paulding County before joining the Maumee River. Bluffs that rise 20-plus feet over the creek in places provide pleasing vistas in a county that is the flattest in the state, northwest Ohio being known for its remarkably consistent flatness. The forested floodplain is also characterized by old oxbows and vernal pools, prime habitat for amphibians, creatures increasingly crowded out of the area over time.

The forest community includes ash, beech, elm, hickory, walnut, sycamore, maple, and a variety of oak trees, with some larger oaks hosting a great blue heron rookery over the years. Over 550 animal and plant species have been documented throughout the preserve with over a dozen of the plant species listed by the state of Ohio as rare, threatened, or endangered. Over 100 bird species, both resident and migratory, have thus far been documented as well.

Plans are to eventually open Forrest Woods to the public as a low-impact nature preserve with only a parking lot, hiking trails, and boardwalk. Deed restrictions prohibit any structure such as a nature center to be built. It will be a place where the magic of the seasons can be sensed and savored be they the soft greens and wildflowers of spring; the darkened hush of a Black Swamp woods in the summer; the riotous colors of a mixed hardwood forest in the fall; or the icy beauty of snow-blanketed woodlands in the winter.

The Forrest Woods Nature Preserve in Paulding County features mature Black Swamp woodlands and a floodplain.

CHAPTER XV

FORTS OF THE MAUMEE RIVER

Stretched along the roughly 100-mile Maumee River Valley from what is now downtown Toledo to downtown Fort Wayne, Indiana, once stood five forts.

Fort Industry

The fort with the oldest and most mysterious roots, however, is one that stood in downtown Toledo on the north bank of Swan Creek at or near its confluence with the Maumee River, Fort Industry.

There once was a plaque affixed to a building at Monroe and Summit streets stating that Fort Industry was built by General Anthony Wayne in 1794 for protection against the British, although this is not true. There is no record of a military fort standing there during Anthony Wayne's 1794 Fallen Timbers campaign, an expedition he mounted from Fort Defiance. During the brief Fallen Timbers campaign, Wayne came no closer to present-day downtown Toledo than the Waterville/Maumee area, and that was only for a few days before heading back to Defiance. There is also no reference to the existence of a Fort Industry in government or military records in the years 1794 to 1804.

What is believed to be true is that a series of French and later British trading posts or supply stations stood on the spot dating back as far as 1670. These posts were no doubt sturdy log structures, designed to protect both the people and goods contained within. It is also probable that these structures were also surrounded by a fence of stakes driven into the ground, or stockade, which would have given the appearance of a fort. When not in use as a trading post or supply station, these structures were likely used as temporary quarters by various passersby, including trappers, soldiers, settlers, and Native Americans. Abandoned by the British in 1796, U.S. soldiers used the site as a temporary outpost in 1803 and 1804.

The one time that Fort Industry does appear in the official record as a "fort" was in 1805 when a treaty was negotiated there with several Indian tribes and signed on July 4th. In the Treaty of Fort Industry the Indians ceded title to roughly 500,000 acres of land in the areas of Erie and Huron counties that came to be known as the Firelands. Whether the fort was a hastily-built stockade constructed strictly for the treaty process or an already existing and improved-upon structure is not known. One of the few references beyond that is in the notes of a state of Ohio surveyor dated Sept. 8, 1805, to a small garrison of U.S. soldiers at "the mouth of Swan Creek," although the name of the post is not given. In succeeding years, the post remained in U.S. government hands, perhaps as late as the War of 1812 when it likely would have been abandoned early in the conflict when the British controlled the region. In January 1813, a force of American troops headed for Frenchtown found the site occupied by Indians and drove them out. After that, Fort Industry faded into the pages of history, with not even a splinter of wood remaining or its precise location known.

However about two hundred years later, an aging, crinkled piece of paper provided a link. A letter cover with a postmark that reads, "Fort Industry, 25 June 1805" was acquired at auction in 2006 by the local history department of the Toledo-Lucas County Public Library. While the letter inside is missing, an inscription on the cover reads "Inclosed is a letter from your Father, in which I presume he has related to you our prospects of success—I feel much better than I did a few hours since—I am in health and good spirits—yours Isaac Mills." Isaac Mills was one of the men present nine days later at the signing of the Treaty of Fort Industry.

A letter cover bearing the postmark of Fort Industry, 1805, was acquired 200 years later by the Toledo-Lucas County Public Library. It represents Toledo's earliest known link with its frontier past.

When Mr. Mills wrote his words that summer day in a frontier outpost that decades later would become downtown Toledo, he couldn't have had any idea that two centuries later his efforts would provide a tangible link between the city and its early frontier past.

Fort Miami

It was late in the morning on August 20, 1794, when a large force of Indian warriors raced for the British Fort Miami on the Maumee River in present-day Maumee. They had just been decisively defeated at the Battle of Fallen Timbers and now were confused, disorganized, and frightened. Inside the walls of the fort, they could find safety and protection with their British "Father." However, what was already a bad day for the

Indians was about to get worse. The British refused to open the gates and the exhausted Indians had to continue their retreat downriver to their camps near Swan Creek. There, they were safe as the Americans broke off their pursuit near the fort.

Fort Miami, officially called Miamis by the British, had been built by them in the spring of that year as a direct result of Anthony Wayne's presence in region. Wayne had spent the previous winter at Fort Greenville in western Ohio and the commander of the British post in Detroit feared that Detroit was Wayne's ultimate destination. No official state of war existed with the United States and England in 1794, but there was no love lost between the two countries in the aftermath of the American Revolution. In fact, Fort Miami stood on territory the British had relinquished to the United States in 1783 after that war.

Now the two countries were facing off again, this time not in Lexington or Concord but in the distant Ohio frontier. Both Anthony Wayne and his British counterpart, Major William Campbell, were under orders to commit no act of war unless sufficiently provoked, which probably was the reason Campbell barred the gates of his fort to the fleeing Indians. Had he admitted the Indians, it is possible Anthony Wayne would have considered this to be provocation and attacked.

Instead what followed was a cat-and-mouse game as Anthony Wayne made camp just out of range of the fort's guns. The next day he and his officers rode within gunshot range for a closer look, a clear insult, and a furious Campbell dispatched a note under a white flag demanding an explanation for their behavior. Wayne replied in so many words that the only explanation the major was entitled to came in the sound of the gunfire he had heard during the previous day's battle at Fallen Timbers. Campbell replied that if the Americans rode within gunshot range of the fort again, he would open fire. Wayne responded by demanding that the British evacuate the fort, due to it being in U.S. territory, and Campbell refused, once more warning Wayne not to approach the fort again.

At this point Anthony Wayne withdrew and on Aug. 23, headed back upriver. He had gotten what he wanted at Fallen Timbers and engaging in miniature replay of the Revolution would not only have been pointless but probably would not have been looked upon favorably by his superiors back east. In addition, the fort would have been very difficult to storm as described by then Lieutenant William Henry Harrison, an aide to Anthony Wayne. An assessment of the fort "showed but too clearly that our small howitzers which had been transported on the backs of the horses, our only artillery, could make no impression upon the massive earthen parapet and the deep fosses and fraising by which it was surrounded afforded no prospect of the success of an escalade." Fosses were moats or ditches while fraising were lines of stout, sharpened sticks that pointed out from the fort almost horizontally.

As things turned out, Anthony Wayne was back at Fort Miami briefly in August 1796 on an inspection tour of western outposts recently turned over by the British to the Americans by way of treaty, Miami included. For the British soldiers of the fort, their two-year stay on the Maumee River had been plagued by inadequate provisions, frontier isolation, and disease, which led to at least a half dozen deaths. Other than a couple of days of drama provided by the presence of Anthony Wayne, boredom must have reigned supreme as well. While the record doesn't indicate this, it is quite possible they were only too glad to turn the fort over.

With no active hostilities with the British or Indians ongoing, the Americans did not stay long and the fort was abandoned, most of its wood likely carried off by settlers for other uses. However the War of 1812 brought military activity back to the Maumee Valley and General William Hull camped at the site in July of that year on his way to his fateful rendezvous in Detroit. The British then used the site as a temporary base in 1813 during the two sieges of Fort Meigs. It was at the site of the old fort during the first siege in May that the Shawnee Chief Tecumseh singularly halted an Indian massacre of American prisoners that was taking place. The British used the site again in July, leaving late in the month, and Fort Miami never again was a place of military activity.

The location today is a preserved historic site open for visitation and while no trace of the physical fort remains, some of the deep ditches or fosses that were dug by the British along the outside walls can clearly be seen.

The deep ditches or "fosses" that fronted the walls of Fort Miami built by the British in 1794 can still be seen in present-day Maumee.

Old Fort Miami

Prior to the existence of the fort the British built in 1794, there was French presence at or near the site of Fort Miami referred to variously as a fort, stockade, trading post, or station that went by the name Miami. The earliest reference to a structure is the year 1680, nearly 100 years prior to the existence of the

United States. The Great Lakes then were in France's domain under the rule of Canadian colonial governor Count de Frontenac who encouraged exploration of the region.

The location is usually given as "the foot of the rapids" where those traveling by boat up the Maumee River find it no longer navigable due to its rocky bottom, a condition that begins in the city of Maumee and exists for about 20 miles to Grand Rapids. The beginning of such rapids would be a logical place to come ashore and build a post. Old French maps refer to a "Port des Miami" or an "F. des Miami" on the Maumee River near the present city of Maumee. Some older histories maintain that the post was on the same spot as the British-built fort and was not only the first, fort-type structure built by white men in what became the state of Ohio, but the first place in the state where France unfurled her flag.

The Fort Miami site is in the 1800 block of River Road at the intersection of Michigan Avenue in Maumee.

Fort Meigs

It was the first week of May 1813 and there was probably no prettier place to witness the wonders of spring than along the high banks of the Maumee River between present-day Perrysburg and Maumee. The soft greens of the emerging leaves on the trees, the spring flowers, and the rushing and rolling rapids of the river would have painted a serene portrait. However, things were anything but serene as thunder roared through the valley, not from a storm but from British cannons raining shells down on Fort Meigs.

Inside the fort, one American soldier had become particularly adept at calling out in what part of the large fort an incoming shell would land, providing precious seconds of warning. The sound of one shell, however, left him confused and silent, a perplexed look on his face. Seconds later that shell landed on him, bringing his time on Earth to an end.

Construction of Fort Meigs began on Feb. 2 and had barely been completed when the British began their bombardment on May 1. General William Henry Harrison, commander of the Army of the Northwest, had selected the spot and out of the ice, snow, and mud rose a large fort where he planned to eventually launch an invasion of Canada. With the loss of Detroit the previous August and a major defeat in the Battle of River Raisin in present-day Monroe, Mich., in January, the war was not going well for the United States in the Northwest Theater. The number of soldiers at the fort would peak at around 2,000.

Now in his newly built fort, Harrison and his army could only hunker down as best they could. Traverses, or protective mounds of earth, ran the length of the fort and along its wings and helped keep the loss of life reasonably low considering the heavy volume of fire, as many as 500 shells a day. Indian snipers crept close and fired into the fort from the ground and from high in trees. However the fort was too well fortified for the British and Indians to make a charge, and the Americans had no intention of leaving its protection to fight on open ground. After about a week, the shelling stopped and the British returned to Ontario.

They would return again in late July. The shelling of the fort this time was not nearly as intense as it was in May, and the second siege of Fort Meigs ended as did the first. On Sept. 10, Commodore Oliver Hazard Perry captured the British fleet in the Battle of Lake Erie and the way to Canada was now open. Harrison ordered the fort reduced in size to a small stockade and left for Canada, leaving behind 100 soldiers to stand guard over the Maumee Rapids. On Oct. 5, Harrison and his army defeated the British and Indians at the Battle of Thames in Ontario and war would never again visit northwest Ohio.

The role of Fort Meigs in the War of 1812 was pivotal and intense, but in terms of time, relatively brief. No great victory was recorded there, nor any defeat, a reflection of the war itself, perhaps, which most historians regard as a stalemate. The war ended in late 1814 and the following May, with little fanfare, the colors over Fort Meigs were lowered for the final time. The abandoned stockade was later burned, either by the military or by squatters, with the remaining logs carried off by settlers for other uses.

At the time it seemed the fort's story would end there. The site sat empty for decades, and was visited again by an aging

Fort Meigs rose from the ice, snow, and mud during the late winter and early spring, 1813, in present-day Perrysburg. The current fort is the largest restored, stockade fort in North America.

William Henry Harrison who presided over the Great Whig Gathering of 1840 that took place on the grounds in his successful presidential campaign of that year. In the years after that, it was used for grazing cattle and was considered sacred ground by local residents. The state of Ohio began acquiring the land in 1907 and following year Civil War veterans dedicated an 82-foot granite obelisk to "the hardy men of 1812-1813." The Ohio Historical Society took over management of the site in 1948 and in 1975 completed a restoration of the fort as originally built in 1813. A second restoration and addition of a museum and education center was dedicated in 2003, coinciding with the state's bicentennial. Fort Meigs is the largest restored, stockade fort in all of North America.

Fort Meigs is located at 29100 River Rd. (State Route 65) in Perrysburg. The fort is open April through October and the museum is open year-round. For more information, call 419-874-4121 or 800-283-8916 or visit www.fortmeigs.org.

Fort Defiance

It was a tired group of soldiers who began building Fort Defiance the 8th of August, 1794, on high ground above the confluence of the Maumee and Auglaize rivers where the city of Defiance now stands. They had been on the march nearly two weeks through west-central Ohio moving a large amount of arms and equipment, most of that time through the Great Black Swamp.

But they and their commander, General Anthony Wayne, were on a mission and that mission was to decisively defeat the Indians in battle on the Ohio frontier. Just prior to their arrival, the confluence was home to a sprawling Indian village but the thousands living there fled in advance of the soldiers' arrival. The major portions of the fort were completed by Aug. 14 and of his bastion Anthony Wayne said, "I defy the English, the Indians and all the devils in Hell to take it."

Wayne and his army left the fort and marched down the Maumee River the next day for their eventual destiny at Fallen Timbers on the 20th, returning about a week later. There would be no rest, however, as Anthony Wayne believed a counterattack from a combined Indian and British force was possible if not probable. Over the next couple of weeks the fort was reinforced with heavy timber, enabling it to withstand bombardment by the largest of British cannons. In the aftermath of Fallen Timbers the British, in fact, actively encouraged the Indians to attack Fort Defiance, offering them arms and gunpowder to do so. However with the British unwilling to play a direct role in any such action, no attack ever came.

On Sept. 14, 1794, Anthony Wayne and the majority of the soldiers headed for Indiana and the headwaters of the Maumee River to build Fort Wayne, leaving a small garrison behind. Fort Defiance was solidly built and designed to be the first line of defense between Wayne's army and the British and Indians, a line that ultimately would not be needed. One who remained at the fort was Joseph Gardner Andrews, a Harvard-educated schoolmaster, working as a surgeon's mate. He kept a daily journal in 1795 that gives an idea of what life was like in a frontier fort located beyond the edge of what was then civilization.

The year began with a New Year's celebration and a feast, although the fare after that was unpredictable and at times scanty, relying on supplies brought by civilian contractors, who appeared sporadically, and on what game could be gathered near the fort. At times supper consisted of "a solitary morsel of poor corn beef," while at others, "venison, pheasants & raccoons; rice pudding & squirrel pye; bacon and eggs; & a boiled flour pudding." In mid-January a party was sent to gather Indian corn from snow-covered fields that had not been harvested in the wake of Fallen Timbers. About that same time the frozen bodies of two American soldiers that had been discovered a few miles away were pulled on sleds into the fort. They were believed to have died from exposure while making their way downriver after deserting from Fort Wayne.

The day-to-day business of the fort for Joseph Andrews consisted of dealing with the sick, of which there was a steady supply. For the commanders of the fort, daily business was dealing with disciplinary issues and with visitors, white and Indian, who came by the fort. Late in the month the Shawnee Chief Blue Jacket, who led the Indian forces at Fallen Timbers, came to the fort with a group making overtures of peace.

In late February a small group of Shawnees stopped by with a white man who had been captured and adopted at such a young age he had forgotten his native language. In March, a young man, half Indian and half French, came to the fort. His fluency in French, English, and five Indian languages made him valuable as an interpreter. By now there were about 70 Indians near the fort, making sugar from maple trees and wanting to know if they could plant crops later in the spring, permission for which was granted.

In April a soldier came to the fort, claiming he had been captured by Indians two years earlier near a fort in southern Ohio and recently escaped. Several days later it was learned from a Shawnee that the soldier was actually a deserter. He was taken into custody and forwarded to Fort Wayne for trial. In May, a Shawnee came to the fort who claimed to be 130 years old. Joseph Andrews, judging from his appearance, figured him to be closer to 40. The month of May also found the soldiers planting vegetable gardens.

The first of June brought a visit from the Miami Chief Little Turtle, leader of Indian forces in American defeats in 1790 and 1791, but who had declined to lead at Fallen Timbers when he saw the handwriting on the wall. Joseph Andrews wrote of him, "his deportment is modest and manly—his visage is marked with penetration—he never gets intoxicated." The next day Little Turtle visited the vegetable gardens with the officers of the fort. There, his mood became melancholy as he observed that the land they were standing on had once belonged to his people. As the month wore on, large numbers of Indians were stopping by the fort, on their way south to Fort Greenville for negotiations of the Treaty of Greenville in July.

On the first of July, Joseph Andrews made a mosquito-plagued journey to Fort Wayne by boat and celebrated the Fourth of July there. With 15 states now in the union, the evening's celebration included the drinking of 15 toasts, followed by 150 artillery rounds and concluding with 15 shells. Andrews returned to Fort Defiance later in the month where a Shawnee chief named Red Pole arrived with 140 members of his tribe and invited those at the fort to watch them dance. "It is very pleasing to observe their regularity & exactness in their motions," Andrews wrote.

In August, the first anniversary of Fallen Timbers was celebrated on the 20th with extra rations of whiskey and a meal of roasted pig and fried chicken. Two days later Joseph Andrews came down with the ague, the dreaded, late summer/early fall malarial fever of the Great Black Swamp, the symptoms of which could last for weeks. On the 27th he treated himself with "9 wine glassfulls of bark & whiskey before dinner," (cinchona bark is a source of quinine, a treatment for malaria) and pronounced himself symptom-free by the end of the day.

As September wore on, more soldiers became ill, Andrews symptoms returned, the bark ran low and the whiskey ran out. The number of sick continued to grow and in October, word was received that upwards of 500 were sick at Fort Greenville and that there was so much sickness at the British Fort Miamis, they were unable to post a single sentry. Joseph Andrews was sick the entire month, on some days too ill to attend to his surgeon's mate duties.

In November a private deserted, and a Shawnee named Nekskorweter living at the fort, who had earned the confidence of the command, was dispatched after him with the promise of $10 if he brought him back alive, and $20 if he returned with his scalp. He soon caught up with the private who refused to turn around and accompany him back to the fort. Nekskorweter shot him in the back, finished the job with a rock, and scalped him. He returned to the fort with his prize and was rewarded both financially and with compliments from the officers. Such was the contempt with which deserters were held.

In December, Christmas was celebrated with a meal of calves head, roasted chickens, veal, chicken pies, pancakes, and a number of bottles of London port wine. The meal was followed by artillery fire. "We then returned & Passed the Evening at our Quarters in drinking and smoking till about 10 oClock; & what is remarkable that on this occasion not a man was intoxicated," Joseph Andrews wrote.

It was the second and last Christmas celebrated by American soldiers at Fort Defiance. In the aftermath of the Treaty of Greenville, area Indians were no longer hostile for the most part and in June 1796 the fort was abandoned. In 1808, a missionary passing by reported that only a few ruins remained from what once was Fort Defiance.

The preserved site of Fort Defiance with historical plaques and markers is located adjacent to the Defiance County Library on Fort Street in Defiance.

Fort Defiance was built on a high point of land at the confluence of the Maumee and Auglaize Rivers in present-day Defiance by General Anthony Wayne in 1794.

Fort Wayne

Like Fort Defiance, Fort Wayne was also built at a confluence of rivers, that of the St. Marys and St. Joseph which combine to form the Maumee River in present-day downtown Fort Wayne. Anthony Wayne arrived there Sept. 17, 1794, from Fort Defiance with over 3,000 soldiers. Despite his victory at Fallen Timbers, peace was far from certain and he ordered the construction of a "regular fortification" instead of a standard, picketed fort.

This meant several extra weeks of hard labor from men already on reduced rations which led to some desertions, despite a report that a previous group of deserters had been caught and killed by Indians. For Anthony Wayne, the lack of adequate provisions was "a constant source of embarrassment, anxiety of mind & distress to me by ten fold more than all the savages in the wilderness."

The fort was nearing completion after about four weeks despite the provision problem, rainy weather, and a bit of rebellious behavior on the part of the troops. It was dedicated on Oct. 22, the anniversary of an American defeat near the site in 1790. Five days later, Anthony Wayne and the bulk of his legion left for Fort Greenville, leaving General John Hamtramck in command. His first order was to name the new garrison Fort Wayne.

For General Hamtramck and the troops of the fort, life at Fort Wayne was similar to that of Fort Defiance; one of frontier isolation at the end of a tenuous supply line. He wrote to an officer friend at Fort Greenville of the solitary nature of life there and, "may you never be obliged to Drink Bad whiskey as we are here and by all means let me know by the first opportunity all the Newse you have." Discipline amongst the rank and file was a constant problem with courts martial a regular feature. At one point Hamtramck wrote to Anthony Wayne, "I am obliged to inform your excellency of the great propensity many of the soldiers have to larceny. I have flogged them until I am tired."

Unlike Defiance and other western Ohio forts that were abandoned in the aftermath of the Treaty of Greenville, Fort Wayne was maintained because of its strategic location and as a center for Indian affairs. Rebuilt in 1800, it would see its most dramatic moments during the War of 1812. Detroit, Fort Mackinac in northern Michigan, and Fort Dearborn (Chicago) had all fallen to British and Indian forces that summer and in late August/early September a force of 500 or more Indians set siege to the Fort Wayne, hurling both gunfire and flaming arrows. At the time, the fort had only about 70 able-bodied soldiers. Added to the garrison's woes was the behavior of the captain in command of the fort who, throughout the siege, "stayed drunk as a fool and perfectly incapable of exercising rationality on any subject whatever," which left the bulk of the command decisions to two lieutenants.

But the soldiers persevered as the Indians were reluctant to storm the fort without British backing, help which never arrived. The siege ended Sept. 12 when General William Henry Harrison arrived with a force of over 2,000. One of the civilians in the fort during the siege was Benjamin F. Stickney who was working as a government Indian agent. He would later become one of the pioneer citizens of Toledo and a player in the so called "Toledo War" in 1835. After the siege, Fort Wayne was not attacked again during the War of 1812, after which its military importance declined.

A third fort was built at the site in 1815-16 and abandoned in 1819. For 25 years there was a working fort at the confluence of the St. Marys and St Josephs which was more years than the other forts of the Maumee River combined.

There is a replica of the third fort at the site now at Historic Fort Park in downtown Fort Wayne. For more information, visit www. oldfortwayne.org.

A replica of the third of three forts named Fort Wayne stands at the headwaters of the Maumee River in downtown Fort Wayne, Indiana.

CHAPTER XVI

THE FIRELANDS

It was a September morn in 1781 during the American Revolution in the bustling seaport city of New London, Connecticut, when the British came to call. The British had been terrorizing parts of the state for several years with a scorched earth policy and New London was going to be next. Within hours, fire roared through the town burning everything in sight, homes, schools, churches, and businesses while from the storehouses along the wharves flowed rum and Irish butter melted by the heat.

New London was the last of nine Connecticut towns, along with nearby farms, that were reduced to ashes and those that lived there, known as the "Sufferers," beseeched the government for new lands upon which to rebuild. Metaphorically, the smoke from those fires drifted all the way to Ohio as the 500,000 acre square of land that they were granted lay at the western end of what was known as the Connecticut Western Reserve. Specifically, it was on the southern shore of Lake Erie in what is now Huron and Erie counties as well as bits of Ottawa and Ashland counties. These lands became known as the Firelands.

However with the land being 700 miles away and mostly uncharted wilderness, and with bureaucracy moving the way it does, it was a full generation or more before actual settlement started taking place. The half million acres were surveyed into five-mile square "towns" which were then subdivided into four sections. These were then distributed by lottery to ensure no one received all good or bad locations.

It wasn't until about 1808 that settlers began to arrive and very few of the original Sufferers made it to Ohio. Many had died or had gotten too old to start over while others sold their claims, some to speculators for a pittance under the duress of poverty brought by the British flames. However when those Connecticut Yankees, their descendants, or those they sold their claims to *did* come, they brought a bit of New England with them. The names of towns and townships in the Firelands include: Norwich, Norwalk, Greenwich, Danbury, Oxford, Lyme, Fairfield, New Haven, and New London. More than just names, they brought architecture as well and perhaps no Firelands town reflects this better than the handsome town of Milan in Huron County with its New England-style town square.

In addition to its layout and architecture, Milan was once home to a bustling, inland port as well as birthplace and childhood home to a true American genius, Thomas Edison, born in 1847. Milan's port days began on July 4, 1839, when the Milan Canal opened. Short, only three miles in length, it was long in terms of commerce because it connected the town to the deeper and navigable section of the Huron River and on to Lake Erie. The canal was a virtual overnight success and wagons bringing in produce and goods for export were at times lined up for several miles waiting to unload.

Though his family moved away when he was only seven, Milan's bustling days left an impression on Thomas Edison as he wrote in a letter to the *Sandusky Register* newspaper in 1922: "I remember wheat elevators on the canal and the Gay Shipyard; also the landing of new boats on which occasion the piece of land called the "Hogback" would be filled with what seemed to be the entire population of the town. I also recall a public square filled at times with farmer's teams and with what seemed to be an immense number of teams that came to town bringing oak staves for barrels. I can just remember seeing a number of Prairie Schooners encamped in front of our house. This was about 1849 or 1850 when I was but a mere infant, and learned afterward that these Prairie Schooners were carrying adventurers to California to hunt for gold."

On Oct. 14, 1846, a supremely confident *Milan Tribune* wrote, "No point on the Great Lakes where so much produce arrives by teams as at Milan, except perhaps Chicago. What is more, it will not only be permanent, but must annually increase, with increased production. We repeat; the coast is clear—the skies are bright, and we see no room for despondency or misgivings."

Indeed the coast was clear and the skies were bright, for a few more years anyway. The following year on May 18, a record 20,000 bushels of grain were brought by wagon to port, and an estimated 650 wagon teams jammed the town on that day. But while the wagons were drawn by horse it would be a different kind of horse, an iron one, that would slowly doom the Milan Canal. In 1851, the amount of wheat shipped through Milan was about a quarter of what it had been in 1847. Not only did railroads put slow end to the canal era everywhere, but when the first rail lines laid in the Firelands area bypassed the town of Milan, both its canal and its importance as a transportation center drifted into history. The story of what once was the southernmost port on the Great Lakes was both spectacular and brief.

The Mad Miller of Milan

One of the early businessmen in Milan was Samuel Winchester, an eccentric who owned a mill with his brother. He was fascinated with the idea of balloon flight and for years carried on a succession of expensive and usually futile experiments. At one point he accidentally set fire to the mill trying to fill his balloon with hydrogen, much to the amusement of the residents of the town, who proclaimed him "the mad miller of Milan." One whose interest he caught was a small boy with a bright and curious mind named Thomas Edison who was repeatedly scolded and sent home for peeking through windows and cracks in doors of the mill, trying to see what was going on.

In 1855 Samuel Winchester finally dragged his rubber coated balloon with its dangling basket to the public square and achieved flight, flying nearly to Fremont before an abrupt wind shift flung him into a tree. Buoyed by his success he made the necessary repairs and planned a second trip, this time from the Huron County seat of Norwalk.

On Oct. 2 of that year he rose from Earth as a band played, a cannon fired, and the women waved their handkerchiefs while the men waved their hats. As he disappeared from view he could be seen triumphantly waving his flag in return, a "madman" proving his critics wrong. The wind took him east and he was seen passing over the village of Berlinville. From there he sailed into immortality as he was never seen again. The newspapers of the day speculated that he was downed in Lake Erie, or in the Canadian wilderness, or perhaps that he even made it as far as the Atlantic Ocean. His fate was never learned.

From the area known as the Firelands came the great American inventor

Thomas Edison, born in Milan in the house above in 1847.

The Connecticut heritage of those who settled the Firelands is reflected in the New England style town square found in Milan.

CHAPTER XVII

SNAPSHOTS

Hull's Trace

It was June 1812 and the Great Black Swamp was in early summer splendor. In the wooded areas, majestic trees towered toward blue skies as puffy white clouds rolled past. In the open parts, marsh grasses waved in the breeze as water, several feet deep in places, shimmered in the sun. And the whole was shrouded in its usual silence, save for the call of a bird, the chatter of a squirrel, or the wind rustling the leaves.

But this June was different as the stillness gave way to the shouts and curses of men, the groans of pack animals, and the crashing of trees being felled as a 2,500-man army, under General William Hull, forced its way through the pristine swamp en route to Detroit. Logs, brush, and trees were removed, the latter being used for corduroy roads in low-lying land. The "road" they cut would come to be known as Hull's Trace as the settlers that came afterward did not think it worthy of the designation of road.

The exact route taken will never be known but according to historical accounts, the army left Urbana on June 16 and entered northwest Ohio, bogging down in the mud near what is today the southern Hancock County line. There they built Fort Necessity before continuing on. They reached the Blanchard River where Main Street crosses the river in

Findlay now, built Fort Findlay, then continued north entering the Black Swamp and present-day Wood County and traveled along Rocky Ford Creek for a bit. From there they made camp near the center of the county on the north branch of the Portage River near the present-day village of Portage, south of Bowling Green.

Some accounts say Hull built "Fort Portage" there but he may have merely used an existing structure. "Where was Fort Portage?" asked the *Bowling Green Sentinel* newspaper in an 1891 article. "Probably not one person in Wood County today is aware that such a fort ever existed." The paper sent a query to an early pioneer whom roamed the area as a youth, Colonel Dresden Howard, who responded: "The Block House you speak of I have passed many times when a boy and camped near its walls and always thought it an old French trader's fort; yet it was near one of the trails used by Hull's army. . . . Hull may have built the block house, as I have often heard the story from older Indians that the 'White Chief' [Hull] had left some of his sick and foot-sore soldiers in a small stockade in the swamp who returned south over the trail." Years later, the story goes, a young woman named Sarah Parshall was walking on the family farm near Portage when she came across a freshly fallen tree. In the top of the tree were 40 muskets, ostensibly stashed by Hull's men.

From the Portage River the army continued north through present-day Bowling Green, along where now lies the railroad track that runs along the western edge of the Bowling Green State University campus. They then angled slightly northwest, passing just west of high ground that is now Union Hill Cemetery. From there the band passed east and north of the present village of Haskins. From there it was a short hike to the Maumee River where they crossed on June 30th to the Lucas County side at Presque Isle Hill and where months later General Winchester and his army would camp. There once was an historical marker at that location—Hull's Crossing— which is no longer there today.

The road cut by Hull and his army was certainly crude but it was the first south-to-north route cut through the breadth of the Black Swamp—Anthony Wayne had a cut a shorter

An old monument on the southern Hancock County line marks where General William Hull entered northwest Ohio on his ill-fated mission to Detroit in June 1812. An inscription on the marker notes the nearby location of Fort Necessity and of an old spring. The stone was placed by the Fort McArthur and Fort Findlay chapters of the Daughters of the American Revolution in 1915.

one through the western portion in 1794 en route to Defiance. The route was used in August by a relief expedition headed for Detroit, which quickly used it again to beat a hasty retreat when Detroit was surrendered by Hull before they arrived. The opening through the woods made by Hull's Trace was used by early settlers to reach interior areas of the swamp and was visible for decades until the land was cleared for farming.

The Old German Church

On a quiet, Williams County road that time seems to have forgotten there stands today Emmanuel Methodist Episcopal Church, built by its members in 1869. The church reaches back to 1842 when the Reverend Riemenschneider preached to a few pioneer German families in a local log cabin home. In 1851, a small frame church was built on the site which served for 18 years until the present brick church was constructed. The congregation passed into the English M.E. Church in 1899 and in 1906 merged with that of the M.E. Church in the nearby village of West Unity. Since then, the church has stood mostly silent, save for an occasional wedding, funeral, or special service, and has served as a chapel for the surrounding Floral Grove Cemetery.

Although time has weathered its brick walls and wooden shutters, this historic house of worship has otherwise changed little over the years. Sunlight slants through the shutters, lighting the wooden pews while a large, glass chandelier, its 16 lamps once fueled by kerosene, hangs from the ceiling. On the altar is a German Bible that dates to 1860 and a pump organ stands nearby. Here, the modern amenities of electricity, central heat, and running water won't be found. And the two entrances to the sanctuary mark a time when men and women entered, and sat, separately.

Despite not being used on a regular basis for over a century, the structure is in good condition as dedicated local residents have raised funds and performed needed repairs and maintenance over the decades. The church, located on County Road K about one mile east of State Route 191 southeast of West Unity, is open to the public during daylight hours from mid-April through mid-October.

The interior of the Emmanuel Methodist Episcopal Church is little changed since it was built in 1869. It stands on a quiet, country road near the village of West Unity in Williams County.

Hopewell Indian Mounds

Tucked into the far corner of northwest Ohio is a reminder of the area's ancient history, the Nettle Lake Mound Group. Hopewell Indians constructed these mounds approximately 2,000 years ago on a plain above Nettle Lake in Williams County. The tribe was known for its large earthworks and burial mounds.

The Hopewell in Ohio lived predominantly in the central and southern parts of the state and left major mound groups near Chillicothe and Newark. They were an established people in eastern North America by about 200 B.C., a culture that lasted about seven centuries. A small part of that culture lived for a time in northwest Ohio on Nettle Lake, leaving behind mounds as silent testimony to their existence. The mounds are the most northern known in the state of Ohio.

Hopewell Indian mounds were built approximately 2,000 years ago near Nettle Lake in Williams County. They are the most northern mounds known in the state of Ohio.

The four mounds range from one to three feet in height and 18 to 30 feet in diameter. And like most Indian mounds, they were improperly excavated by relic hunters in the past. However a 1968 dig by the Ohio Historical Society found flake knives, pottery pieces, and ashes, chipped flint and burned rocks, possibly from a cremation. A 1988 excavation along nearby Nettle Creek sponsored by the Williams County Historical Society and the University of Toledo found artifacts dating from 8,000 B.C. to 1,200 A.D. The site was entered into the National Register of Historic Places in 1974.

Along the northern edge of the site lies a different and much more recent bit of history, an old stagecoach road that ran between Hillsdale, Michigan, and Fort Wayne, Indiana. Then as now, travelers must have pulled off the road for a time to wander among the mounds and wonder who built them there.

The Nettle Lake Mound Group is located on County Road 4-75 west of Nettle Lake. The site is open dawn to dusk, May through October. The Williams County Historical Society in Montpelier maintains a large display of Hopewell artifacts in its museum on the Williams County Fairgrounds.

Ancestors

Pictured on page 125 is the J. W. Whitmer Dry Goods Store on West Wayne Street in Maumee with a sign announcing that Joseph Mollenkopf was assuming proprietorship. Joseph was the author's great-grandfather. The photo is not dated, however he died in July 1887 at the age of 25, after undergoing an unsuccessful kitchen table appendectomy according to family lore, so the photograph predates 1887.

The woman standing to his left was his wife and the author's great-grandmother Ella Mollenkopf. She never remarried and struggled after his death, raising two young children on her own, and became a writer for a Cleveland religious paper. She later joined the staff of *The Blade* around 1900 at a time when women were few in newsrooms and those that were, were not allowed to cover "hard" news. However she received an opportunity when there was a drowning of a party of young people and, with no male reporters available, covered the event, getting the only interview with a survivor and scooping rival papers. She was rewarded by being made a general assignment reporter and thus became, it is believed, the first female news correspondent in Toledo. She lived until 1948.

The building that once housed the dry goods store still stands at 107 W. Wayne St. in Maumee.

A young merchant named Joseph Mollenkopf and his wife Ella, stand-ing to his left, pose in front of their newly acquired dry goods store on West Wayne Street in Maumee in the mid 1880s. The identity of the others in the photo is not known.

ABOUT THE AUTHOR

Jim Mollenkopf is a Toledo, Ohio, author and photographer. A former social worker and newspaper reporter, this is his sixth book. He previously wrote and published: *Lake Erie Sojourn: an autumn tour of the parks, public places, and history of the lake erie shore*; *The Great Black Swamp: historical tales of 19th century northwest ohio*; *The Great Black Swamp II: more historical tales of northwest ohio*; *Civil War Stories of Northwest Ohio Heroes*; and *Great Black Swamp Woods & Wanders: Nature's Jewels in Northwest Ohio.*

REFERENCES

Andrews, Joseph G. *A Surgeon's Mate at Fort Defiance.* Richard C. Knopf (ed.). Columbus: Ohio Historical Society, 1957.

Altoff, Gerard T. *Oliver Hazard Perry and the Battle of Lake Erie.* The Perry Group: Put-in-Bay, OH, 1999.

Au, Dennis. *War on the Raisin: A Narrative Account of the War of 1812 in the River Raisin Settlement, Michigan Territory.* Monroe County (Michigan) Historical Commission, 1981.

Bald, Clever F. "Fort Miami." *Northwest Ohio Quarterly* 15 (1943): 127-138.

Barr, Daniel P. "A Monster So Brutal: Simon Girty and the Degenerative Myth of the American Frontier, 1783-1900." *Essays in History*, Vol. 40. University of Virginia, 1998.

Berton, Pierre. *The Invasion of Canada.* Boston: Little, Brown and Co., 1980.

Bowersox, Charles A. *A Standard History of Williams County, Ohio.* Chicago: Lewis Publishing Co., 1920.

Britsch, Carl Conrad. *The Sound of the Hammer.* New York: Vantage Press, 1963.

Brown, Samuel R. *Views of the Campaign of the Northwestern Army.* Burlington, VT: Samuel Mills, 1814.

Buchman, Randall L. *The Confluence.* Defiance: The Defiance College Press, 1994.

Bunnell, David C. *The Travels and Adventures of David C. Bunnell.* Palmyra, NY, 1931.

Burnet, Jacob. *Notes on the Early Settlement of the North-Western Territory*. Cincinnati: Derby, Bradley & Co., Publishers: 1847.

Butterfield, Consul W. *History of the Girtys*. Cincinnati: Robert Clarke & Co., 1890.

Carpenter, Helen M. "The Origin and Location of the Firelands of the Western Reserve." *The Ohio State Archeological and Historical Quarterly*. Vol. 64, No. 2 (April 1935):163-203.

Cass, Lewis A. (ed.). *History of Henry and Fulton Counties, Ohio*. D. Mason & Co., Publishers, 1888.

Clift, Glenn G. *Remember The Raisin*. Frankfort, KY: Kentucky Historical Society, 1961.

Darnell, Elias. *A Journal Containing an Accurate and Interesting Account*. Philadelphia: Lippincott, Grambo and Co., 1854.

Faben, W. W. "Old Settlers' Tales: Stories of Williams County." *Northwest Ohio Quarterly*. Vol. 28 (Spring 1956): 109-112.

Font, Walter (ed.). *A Garrison at Miami Town*. Allen County-Fort Wayne Historical Society, 1994.

Frohman, Charles E. *Milan and the Milan Canal*. Sandusky, NP: 1976.

Grieser, Orland R. and Beck, Ervin. *Out of the Wilderness*. The Dean-Hicks Co., Grand Rapids, MI, 1960.

Howlett, W.J. *Life of the Right Reverend Joseph P. Machebeuf, D.D.* Pueblo Co: The Franklin Press Co., 1908.

Ingham, John B. *Simon Girty: Degeneration Through Violence*. M.A. Thesis, Bowling Green State University, 1981.

Ketcham, Wilmont. "Cedar Point in Light of Other Days." *Northwest Ohio Quarterly* Vol. 9, January 1937.

Keeler, Ralph. *Vagabond Adventures*. Boston: Fields, Osgood & Co., 1870.

Lorrain, Alfred M. *The Helm, The Sword and The Cross: A Life Narrative*. Cincinnati: Poe & Hitchcock, 1862.

Lossing, Benson. *The Pictorial Fieldbook of the War of 1812*. New York: Harper and Brothers, 1868.

Meckley, Robert C. *Keeping Faith With Themselves: Indian Ritual and the Battle of the River Raisin*. M.A. Thesis, Miami (Ohio) University, 1992.

Mollenkopf, Fred P. *The German Immigration of Toledo, Lucas County and Northwest Ohio*. M.A. Thesis, The University of Toledo, 1991.

Nelson, Larry L. *Men of Patriotism, Courage, & Enterprise! Fort Meigs in the War of 1812*. Canton, OH: Daring Press, 1985.

Paine, Albert Bigelow. *Mark Twain: A Biography*. New York: Harper & Brothers Publishers, 1912.

Quaife, Milo M. (ed.). *The Indian Captivity of O.M. Spencer*. New York: The Citadel Press, 1968.

Reighard, Frank H. *A Standard History of Fulton County, Ohio*. Chicago: The Lewis Publishing Co., 1920.

Ryan, James A. *The Town of Milan. Sandusky*, NP, 1928.

Sherman, Walter J. "Old Fort Industry and the Conflicting Historical Accounts." *Northwest Ohio Quarterly*, Vol. 2 (July 1930).

Sherman, Walter J. "Fort Miami—At the Foot of the Rapids of the Miami of the Lake." *Northwest Ohio Quarterly* Vol. 9, July 1937.

Slocum, Charles E. *History of the Maumee River Basin*. Bowen & Slocum: Indianapolis and Toledo, 1905.

Spitzer, Carl B. "Construction and Physical Appearance of Fort Miami." *Northwest Ohio Quarterly*, Vol. 16 (April 1944): 112-116.

Van Tassel, Charles S. *Story of the Maumee Valley, Toledo and the Sandusky Region*, Vol. 1. Chicago: S.G. Clarke Publishing, 1929.

Van Gundy, Paul. *Stories of the Fountain City*. Bryan, OH: The Bryan Area Foundation, 1975.

Wallace, Lee, Jr. "The Petersburg Volunteers, 1812-1813." *The Virginia Magazine of History*, Vol. 82, 1979.

Williams, W.W. *History of the Firelands*. Cleveland, Leader printing Co., 1879.

Winchester, James. *Historical Details Having Relation to the Campaign of the Northwestern Army Under General Harrison*. Lexington, KY: Worsley & Smith, Printers, 1818.

Woehrmann, Paul. *At the Headwaters of the Maumee*. Indianapolis: Indiana Historical Society, 1971.

_____ *Anecdotes of the Lake Erie Area: War of 1812*. Richard C. Knopf (ed.). Columbus: Anthony Wayne Parkway Board, 1957.

_____*Sandusky County Pioneer and Historical Society Yearbook. Proceedings of Its 30th Reunion*. Fremont, OH. Sterling Printing, 1918.

Newspaper articles

"Caused by a Drunken Son." *The New York Times*, December 26, 1880.

"Events of the War." *The (Niles) Weekly Register*, March 6, 1813.

"Ex-Gov. Scott Acquitted." *The New York Times*, November 6, 1881.

"Fort Portage." *The Bowling Green Sentinel*, ND.

"Missing: Ralph Keeler Supposed to Have Been Lost at Sea." *Toledo Daily Blade*, December 29, 1873.

"Napoleon's Woe." *The (Napoleon) Democratic Northwest*, December 30, 1880.

"Pioneer Reminiscences: Early Days in Wood County." *Toledo Daily Blade*, March 13, 1875.

"Toledo's First Public Enemy No. 1." *The Toledo News-Bee*, April 20, 1937.